AN APPEAL TO REASON

Praise for *An Appeal to Reason*

"If you are a trial lawyer, you need to read this book - long *before* you go to trial! Donna Bader's new book, *An Appeal to Reason*, is filled with practical tips and advice that will help you create and protect the record for appeal, dramatically increasing your odds of success in this uncertain arena."

Joane Garcia-Colson
Trial Consultant and Trial Lawyer
Author of *Trial In Action: The Persuasive Power of Psychodrama*
www.the3sisters.org

"Over the past 25 years I've taken almost every type of case you can imagine to trial and thought I had experienced nearly every conceivable situation that can take place before a jury and in chambers. I thought I knew all the important stuff about avoiding appeal—until I read Donna's book. It's the best guide I've ever seen that shows you exactly what to do to protect the record and avoid appeal by opposing counsel at each stage of trial. The short and concise 'how to' tips are pearls of wisdom that WILL help you win your case and WILL show you how to protect your judgment on appeal. I especially like the quick and easy to review 'Tips for Success.' Every trial lawyer should review this book before starting a new trial. Thomas Jefferson must have penned his famous words, 'information is the currency of democracy' after he read Donna's book!"

Mitch Jackson, Esq.
Jackson & Wilson, Inc.
Orange County Trial Lawyer
Association's 2009
Trial Lawyer of the Year
Laguna Hills, California
www.jacksonandwilson.com

"Donna Bader does it again! She gives attorneys a clear and simple step-by-step guide to help set up their cases for appeal. Her section on 'Creating A Clear Record' echoes what ACT of Communication® has been teaching for decades. And I love her advice to create persuasive arguments that can be delivered over the radio. After all, appellate justices have only words, not visuals, to guide their review of the trial."

Katherine James
Founding Director
ACT of Communication®
Trial Consultants
www.ActofCommunication.com

"Lawyers who have never tried a case should be required to read Donna Bader's book before agreeing to represent a client; lawyers with lots of experience should review it before they begin their next case. Though written for trial lawyers, *An Appeal to Reason* is a valuable resource for appellate lawyers as well. Ms. Bader's list of tips is succinct and informative without condescending to the reader. Her ideas are easy to remember, and implement because she offers authority and identifies appropriate forms to use in every stage of the trial process. I look forward to using *An Appeal to Reason* the next time I teach an appellate practice course."

Wendy Lascher, Esq.
Certified Specialist in Appellate Law
(Cal Bd. Legal Spec.)
Ferguson Case Orr Paterson LLP
Ventura, California
www.fcopc.com

"After an hour with Bader's new book, the nascent appeal lawyer in me says 'clear; cogent; to the point.' *An Appeal to Reason* is the consummate carry-along for the busy law-and-motion and trial lawyer who needs to keep an eye on the possible—god forbid—appeal. Keep it on your smart phone, iPad and laptop. Dip into it before you wade into Witkin, Rutter or Matthew Bender."

Eric J. Schindler, Esq.
McKennon | Schindler LLP
Insurance and
Business Dispute Attorneys
Newport Beach, California
mslawllp.com

"Donna Bader has written a book that will be a wonderful resource for attorneys litigating in both trial and appellate courts. The book concisely highlights the pitfalls in pre-trial, trial and post-trial proceedings that can adversely affect trial and appellate outcomes. Copious case citations are provided and the book will be particularly helpful for trial attorneys who are uncomfortable or unfamiliar with the appellate process. If you are a trial lawyer who wants to maximize the chance that you will prevail in the trial court and position yourself to be successful on appeal, this book belongs on your shelf or computer – and having it on the PDA you take to court wouldn't be a bad idea either."

Barry M. Wolf, Esq.
Law Office of Barry M. Wolf
Certified Specialist, Appellate Law
11150 Olympic Blvd., #1050
Los Angeles, CA 90064
www.wolfappeals.com

"I think this book offers the wise perspective of a seasoned appellate attorney in a reader-friendly format. Each topic gives the reader just enough information to be aware of potential pitfalls without overwhelming details. The cites are particularly helpful and give lawyers a starting point to read further on each topic."

Lori Roberts
Associate Professor of Law and
Director of Professional Skills
Western State University
College of Law
Fullerton, California
www.wsulaw.edu

Also by Donna Bader

California Litigation Series:
California Summary Judgment and Related Termination Motions
(The Rutter Group, 2011)

AN APPEAL TO REASON:

204 STRATEGIC TOOLS TO HELP YOU WIN YOUR APPEAL AT TRIAL

By

Donna Bader

Bench Press Publishing
Laguna Beach, California
www.BenchPressPublishing.com

Printed in the United States of America

ISBN (cloth): 978-0-9836204-0-2

Library of Congress Control Number: 2011907115

Bench Press Publishing
668 North Coast Highway, Ste. 1355
Laguna Beach, California 92651
Tel.: (949) 436-5260
Fax: (949) 494-1017
E-mail: info@BenchPressPublishing.com

Jacket and Interior design by Jason Bader

Edited by Michele Magar, Esq.

Photography by Donna Bader

This book is printed on acid-free paper.

To Tony Klein and Casper,
You have helped make me what I am . . .
and I hope that's a good thing!

Donna

~ TABLE OF CONTENTS ~

Appendices

~ ACKNOWLEDGMENTS ~

While writing a book seems like a solo pursuit, in reality many people have made this book possible. If a lot of clients and attorneys over the past three decades had not trusted me with their appeals, I wouldn't have been in a position to observe firsthand the mistakes that occur in the appellate process. While I never thought of them as guinea pigs, they provided admittance to the forum where I learned appellate law.

There are a number of people who helped by giving me tips and gave me gentle criticism. Thanks to the following individuals: Mitch Jackson, Lisa Wilson, Eric Schindler, Lor Gold, Barry Wolf, Joane Garcia-Colson, Wendy Lascher, Judge Thierry Colaw, Justice Richard Fybel, Lori Roberts, and Katherine James.

Thanks to my family, and especially my mother, who seem to be proud of me, no matter what I do. They may not truly understand how I earn my living, or why I can't seem to do one thing to the exclusion of others, but they have always supported me. It was especially nice to be able to call on the services of my nephew, Jason Bader, who designed my book cover and layout.

Thanks to my friend and editor, Michele Magar, for providing her professional services in editing this book and giving me valuable feedback along the way.

A very special thanks, saved for the last, to Tony Klein, my partner in crime, who viewed this book as a true collaboration. He never withheld his honest opinions, which I value so deeply. He encouraged me every step of the way and made me feel that I had something important to say and give to others. And a special nod to our dog Casper, because he provided the support I needed in times of stress to reduce my blood pressure and to remind me that sometimes you have to take a break to walk the dog.

~ AUTHOR'S NOTE ~

This book is intended for practicing attorneys and contains suggestions that I have gathered over three decades of practicing appellate law. It focuses on the most common mistakes that I have observed throughout my career and is not meant to be a comprehensive treatment of any of the topics covered herein. It also focuses on appellate practice in the California courts. This book does not offer legal advice on any particular case and does not take the place of consultation with an attorney or other professional with appropriate expertise and experience.

Attorneys are strongly cautioned to evaluate the information, ideas and opinions set forth in this book in light of their own research, experience and judgment, to consult applicable rules, regulations, procedures, cases and statutes (including those issued after the publication date of this book), and to make independent decisions about whether and how to apply such information, ideas, and opinions to a particular case. As always, shepardize all cases and statutes before inserting them into any legal documents.

The author disclaims any liability or responsibility for loss or damage resulting from the use of this book or the information, ideas or opinions contained in this book.

~ INTRODUCTION ~

While at a recent dinner party, I was talking to a seasoned trial attorney. When I told him that I was an appellate attorney, he became quite animated. "I don't know anything about appeals!" He announced with unmistakable pride. "I just win my cases and don't worry about appeals."

I could not help but look at him in awe. Yes, I was in awe of his . . . arrogance. Not only was my role in the appellate process ignored – I was unnecessary! – but I was concerned his arrogance might eventually cause his clients to lose their appeals.

His attitude, although taken to an extreme, is not that unusual. I have received calls from trial attorneys asking about appellate procedures. Their common refrain is "I don't handle appeals. It's not my area." While appellate procedure is a specialized area of law and procedure (although one can still find trial attorneys handling their own appeals), it often overlaps into the realm of the trial attorney.

If a client came to a trial attorney to discuss a potential personal injury claim, that attorney would certainly advise the client of the applicable statute of limitations and the final date to file a complaint. In my opinion, the same principle applies *at the end of the case.* Once a judgment has been entered (or even before), the trial attorney should advise the client *in writing* about the deadline for filing an appeal. At a minimum, trial attorneys must understand enough about the appellate process to know the deadlines for filing a notice of appeal. If they ignore what happens after the judgment is rendered, they do so at their peril. I have known of attorneys who were forced to file a notice of appeal and pay the filing fees for a client they no longer wanted to represent.

Trial attorneys need to know the fundamental rules of appellate procedure. They cannot leave it to the appellate attorney because by the time we get involved, it may be too late to raise the issue or preserve the record. The trial attorney is the one who has the opportunity to create the record; appellate attorneys are limited by the trial attorney's creation.

Let's take one of the most fundamental rules of appellate procedure: new issues ordinarily cannot be raised for the first time on appeal. (Yes, of course, there are exceptions but I won't discuss them here.) These "issues" can range from something as simple as failing to object and obtain a ruling on an objection, to ignoring serious misconduct by the court, opposing counsel or the jury when it occurs. They may also include raising new theories of liability, defenses, and damages.

Documents and facts that were not presented below do not become part of the record, and as a consequence, they cannot be considered on appeal. (*Doers v. Golden Gate Bridge, Highway and Transportation District* (1979) 23 Cal.3d 180, 184, fn. 1; *Pulver v. Avco Financial Services* (1986) 182 Cal.App.3d 622, 632.) If the trial attorney decides not to bring out certain facts at trial, the appellate court will never know they existed because the appellate attorney is not allowed to present them.

What does that mean for the trial attorney? It means trial attorneys cannot ignore the need to understand the appellate process. They must learn how to act at the trial court level to protect their clients' rights on appeal. They certainly don't want to find themselves in a situation where they are deemed to have waived their clients' right to object or even invited the error of which they now complain.

I cannot stress the importance of the need for trial attorneys to do their job. Time and time again, I have been retained to work on an appeal, only to discover a point on appeal has been lost due to the acts or omissions of the trial attorney. By saying "lost," I don't mean the issue can be "found" or resurrected. No, it is lost forever. Sometimes it is just one issue of several, but on other occasions, the loss will deal a death blow to the *entire* appeal.

In her *L.A. Times* article, Laura Ernde noted that more and more trial attorneys are turning to appellate attorneys for help *before* there is a final judgment. Appellate attorneys can be of great assistance in fashioning motions *in limine*, jury instructions and special verdict forms. Their focus will be on making sure all appropriate objections are raised and that the record preserves all possible grounds for appeal. One appellate specialist, Jerry Falk, of Howard, Rice, Nemerovski, Canady, Falk & Rabkin in San Francisco, described a case where one of his clients lost a $90 million contract fraud case because of a technicality. By the time Falk got involved, there was nothing he could do.

All of the appellate attorneys interviewed for Ernde's article noted a change in trial preparation in the last ten years as trial attorneys became willing to seek assistance to prevent errors and make sure they adequately preserved the record. She noted that bringing in an appellate specialist at the early stages of trial preparation has become almost "standard practice" at big firms like Reed Smith and Horvitz & Levy in Southern California. Small firms should also incorporate this intelligent planning into their trial preparation. This wisdom applies with equal force in motions that can terminate your case, such as a motion for summary judgment, an anti-SLAPP motion, or even a demurrer.

Having seen far too many trial attorneys ruin any chance for a successful appeal, I've written articles, given training seminars, and spoken frequently on the subject. Warnings may sound great while an attorney is attending a conference, but the lessons are soon forgotten when that attorney returns to his or her daily routine. This book gives trial lawyers the crucial information they need in a format that can be saved and referenced as the issue arises, often in the midst of trial in California state courts. It can make the difference between winning or losing an appeal.

CHAPTER 1. UNDERSTANDING THE ROLE OF ATTORNEYS IN THE APPELLATE PROCESS

An all too familiar scenario: *You've lost at trial. To compound your misery, the judge has ruled against you in post-trial motions. You call your appellate attorney, explaining, "Look, this should be a cheap and easy appeal. After all, I've done all of the research on the case and the authorities are in my post-trial motions. And since I know the facts, I should probably argue the appeal. Unfortunately, there were a few sidebar and chamber conferences that weren't reported. I hope that won't be a problem."*

What's wrong with this picture?

1 All attorneys are not alike.

To fully understand how a trial attorney can assist in the appellate process, one must appreciate the differences between trial lawyers and appellate practitioners. Why is that helpful? Because the appellate attorney can (and should) become part of the trial team and understanding how he or she works will mean more effective communication between team members and an intelligent division of tasks.

2 The trial attorney creates the record.

Until the trial lawyer comes along, there are no transcripts or records. It is up to the trial lawyer to create them. He or she must take a naked set of facts presented by the client and attempt to weave them into a coherent story. This story must be persuasive to a jury or the court. The trial attorneys' work - whether taking depositions, appearing for motions, or trying a case – is done in a public forum. Their success, to a large extent, is dependent on the spoken word. But trial attorneys cannot overlook that at the appellate level the written briefs are much more important than the eventual oral argument. Those written briefs are heavily dependent on presenting a record created by the trial attorney. Thus, unless an appellate attorney is involved at the trial level, it is up to the trial attorney to create a complete and meaningful record.

3 Appreciate the differences between trial and appellate attorneys.

Trial attorneys tend to be risk-takers, especially if they are hired on a contingency basis. They are willing to take cases, knowing there is a possibility they will lose and not get paid (not to mention the expenditure of costs which may never be recovered on the client's behalf). A case may rise or fall on a jury or the court's impressions of the personalities of the attorneys and their clients. Appellate attorneys tend to work far from the glare of the courtroom. Despite the creative flair they may impart to their briefs (or at oral argument), winning or losing is not dependent on the appellate attorney's charisma. Appeals are made to a different audience, one that might not be so easily swayed by emotional pleas. That's why appellate attorneys have often been characterized as the intellectuals or "eggheads" of the legal profession.

4 Appellate attorneys are often limited by the existing record.

Even though appellate attorneys can be creative in fashioning their briefs, they are limited to creating a story or legal argument based on an existing record. They are dependent on (or stuck with) the record created by the trial attorney. In essence, appellate attorneys are usually late to the party while the trial attorney is there from the beginning. All too often, the trial attorney fails to consider the need to create a record that will allow the appellate attorney to make a persuasive argument either in support of or against the findings below. Having an appellate attorney participate in the creation of the record can certainly help to ensure that issues are raised and protected for a later appeal.

5 The role of the appellate attorney is different from that of the trial attorney.

The appellate and trial attorneys have different jobs to do. The trial attorney must present the case to a trier of fact to determine factual questions and must satisfy a legal burden of proof when presenting evidence. The appellate attorney asks the appellate court to decide questions of law but must show prejudicial error.

6 Don't act like a trial attorney if you are handling your client's appeal.

One of the major criticisms I hear from appellate court justices is that trial attorneys who handle their own appeals merely recycle their trial briefs or motions presented below. To compound the problem, these same attorneys appear for oral argument and reargue the evidence as if they were addressing a jury. In *In re Marriage of Shaban* (2001) 88 Cal.App.4th 398, the court described this problem:

> "Appellate work is most assuredly not the recycling of trial level points and authorities. Of course, the orientation of trial work and appellate work is obviously different . . . , but that is only the beginning of the differences that come immediately to mind.
>
> "For better or worse, appellate briefs receive greater judicial scrutiny than trial level points and authorities, because three judges (or maybe seven) will read them, not just one judge. The judges will also work under comparatively less time pressure, and will therefore be able to study the attorney's 'work product' more closely. They will also have more staff (there are fewer research attorneys per judge at the trial level) to help them identify errors in counsel's reasoning, misstatements of law and miscitations of authority, and to do original research to uncover ideas and authorities that counsel may have missed, or decided not to bring to the court's attention."

(*Id.* at pp. 408-409.)

7 Appellate attorneys do not simply recycle the work of the trial attorney.

I know I am dealing with this type of approach when the trial attorney suggests that my job will be easy because I can just take his or her motion for new trial and insert it into the appellate brief. Failing to tailor the appellate brief to the correct audience – which will be apparent to the court of appeal – will not serve the client's interests. Because courts of appeal are not bound by the decisions of other appellate courts, "appellate court precedent is open for reexamination and critical analysis. Along the same lines, appellate counsel must necessarily be more acutely aware of how a given case fits within the overall framework of a given area of law, so as to be able to anticipate whether any resulting opinion will be published, and what effect counsel's position will have on the common law as it is continuously developed." (*In re Marriage of Shaban* (2001) 88 Cal. App.4th 398, 409.) The court in *In re Marriage of Shaban, supra,* concluded:

> "The upshot of these considerations is that appellate practice entails rigorous original work in its own right. The appellate practitioner who takes trial level points and authorities and, without reconsideration or additional research, merely shovels them in to an appellate brief, is producing a substandard product. Rather than being a rehash of trial level points and authorities, the appellate brief offers counsel probably their best opportunity to craft work of original, professional, and, on occasion, literary value."

(*Id.* at p. 410.)

8 Don't reuse a work product that failed to persuade the trial court below.

If I am retained to represent an appellant, I am understandably reluctant to use a work product that has already failed to persuade the trial court. Whatever the trial attorney did below was not successful, so why should I want to repeat those same mistakes or take the same approach? If, on the other hand, I am called on to represent the respondent who won below, I still prefer to make the winning argument in a different manner rather than relying on old paperwork that was addressed to the trial court below. Why not take two opportunities to persuade rather than recycling a single approach? In both cases, the work product must now address a new audience - the court of appeal - which uses a different standard of review.

9 Avoid "shoveling" your old documents filed below into a new document filed at the appellate level.

Some attorneys do not even take that additional step of "shoveling" in an attempt to hide the fact that they are filing recycling documents. In *Parker v. Wolters Kluwer United States, Inc.* (2007) 149 Cal.App.4th 285, the appellant referred to documents he filed with the trial court below and incorporated them by reference into his appellate brief. Now, that takes a lot of chutzpah to be so confident of your position that you don't even have to lay it out for the court. If the justices are interested, let them go find the documents in the record! Not only did the Court of Appeal find this to be a violation of California Rules of Court, rule 8.204(a)(1)(B), but it annoyed them enough to make a published comment and then reject the attorney's "incorporated" arguments. I'll bet his client was not pleased with saving printing expenses as a result of the attorney's abbreviated arguments.

10 An appeal is (almost always) not about credibility.

One of the biggest mistakes that trial attorneys make is viewing the appeal as a second bite at the apple. The appellate court is not the forum for retrying questions of fact or reweighing the evidence. "'Fundamentally, unlike trial, the purpose of an appeal is not to determine the case on its merits, but to review for trial court error.'" (*Uriarte v. United States Pipe & Foundry Co.* (1996) 51 Cal. App.4th 780, 791.) For instance, if a client or the attorney insists, "the witness lied on the stand" or "we had better evidence than they did," I know the client is seeking to retry the case, especially on questions of fact, and credibility will be a major factor. But the court of appeal cannot determine if someone is lying or telling the truth, and will almost always defer to the trier of fact in this area. "Appellate courts 'do not reweigh evidence or reassess the credibility of witnesses.' . . . Put another way, '[t]he Court of Appeal is not a second trier of fact . . .'" (*Marriage of Balcof* (2006) 141 Cal.App.4th 1509, 1531.)

11 Understand what the trial court is communicating to the courts of appeal when it says that a witness or party lacks credibility.

Another frequent area of concern by parties is where the lower court has stated, usually in an order or statement of decision, that the party's testimony lacks credibility. No one wants to have a public record made of a judicial officer's conclusions about the veracity of a party. Unfortunately, that finding is reduced to a written communication to the appellate court of the lower court's impressions of the demeanor and truthfulness of a witness. It is a difficult label to overcome, especially when the court of appeal may never lay its collective eyes on the witness, while the trial court was situated only a few feet away. This problem may not preclude success on appeal if the trial court commits legal error or there is other independent evidence that supports the witness's testimony.

~ Tips for Success ~

- Work as a team with the appellate attorney. Each attorney should have distinct and separate tasks in handling dispositive motions and trial proceedings.

- Enhance effective team communication by understanding each member's skills and roles.

- Value the perspective the appellate attorney can bring to trial preparation and in protecting your client's rights.

- Understand that an appellate attorney does not merely recycle paperwork previously presented to the trial court when preparing an appellate brief.

- Create a meaningful record the appellate attorney can work with in handling an appeal.

- Enlist the assistance of an appellate attorney to help protect the client's rights by making sure the grounds for appeal are preserved at the trial level.

CHAPTER 2. OBSTACLES ATTORNEYS FACE ON APPEAL

An all too familiar scenario: *Even though you lost at trial, you feel confident that the trial court erred in some of its rulings. Rather than objecting at trial, you thought it would be a great strategy to keep silent and then challenge the rulings on appeal. You call your appellate attorney and report the errors in the court's rulings. "This should be an easy appeal. Can't we just show that the court was wrong? For instance, Special Jury Instruction No. 22 should never have been given, even though I asked for a special instruction that was quite similar. Of course, mine was much better. To tell you the truth, I think the trial court's reasoning was wrong, but it probably reached the right decision."*

Did the trial court commit reversible error?

12 Avoid an appeal if at all possible.

If you are representing an appellant, you are going into battle with less than a 50/50 chance of success. Over the years, the courts have published their statistics. While the data differs depending on the standard of review and type of appeal, it does not provide cause for optimism. The chances of obtaining a reversal or other affirmative relief ranges around 15-25%. That means the average appellant faces a 75-85% chance of losing. Those are not great odds. One would certainly not want to go into life-threatening surgery with those odds. Try to avoid an appeal, if at all possible, and consider various post-trial motions that may be available to you so that you can try to win at the trial court level. However, the negative statistics don't necessarily mean appellants can't win on appeal. Obviously, appellants win enough of the time to make an appeal a worthwhile gamble; however, obstacles need to be considered and disclosed to the client. If the client chooses to move forward with the appeal, it will be an informed decision.

13 Know the difference between good and bad appeals.

Appellate practitioners love certain types of appeals. For instance, appeals from dismissals after orders sustaining demurrers and summary judgment offer more promise than an appeal based on the substantial evidence standard of review. There are several reasons for this:

- Usually the record is not as large and the issues are limited.
- There is a better chance for reversal because the courts will carefully scrutinize the termination of a case that deprives a party of a trial on the merits.

- The appellant doesn't have to worry about a jury making a factual determination or the trial court exercising its discretion.
- The standard for review is an independent or de novo review, meaning the court of appeal will review the record as if the trial court never existed.

14 As a starting point, judgments are presumed to be correct.

While this sounds like one of those basic principles that we learn in law school, such as the liberal construction of a complaint that is challenged by demurrer, this principle must be considered as an obstacle in an appeal. Think about it – judgments are presumed correct. Sounds simple, but what it means is that whenever a justice picks up your brief and starts to read, that is his or her mindset. They have been instructed to preserve the judgment if possible. It works something like a presumption of guilt except that you, as the appellant, are considered to be wrong and the court right. Of course, it makes good sense because if judgments were not governed by this presumption or presumed incorrect, then everyone would be running to the courthouse to challenge an adverse result. The courts are burdened enough as it is; remember, in 75-85% of the cases the courts of appeal affirm the judgment as correct. This principle is aptly expressed in *Denham v. Superior Court of Los Angeles County* (1970) 2 Cal.3d 557:

> "[I]t is settled that: 'A judgment or order of the lower court is *presumed correct.* All intendments and presumptions are indulged to support it on matters as to which the record is silent, and error must be affirmatively shown. This is not only a general principle of appellate practice but an ingredient of the constitutional doctrine of reversible error.'"

(*Id.* at p. 564; italics in original.) (See also *State Farm Fire & Casualty Co. v. Pietak* (2001) 90 Cal. App.4th 600, 610.)

15 **It is the appellant's burden to produce a meaningful record.**

The "record" consists of (1) the Clerk's Transcript or an appendix of documents filed with the trial court and prepared by one or more of the parties, (2) the Reporter's Transcript of the oral proceedings, and (3) the exhibits. If you are the appellant, you have the burden of showing error on an adequate record. (*Iliff v. Dustrud* (2003) 107 Cal.App.4th 1201, 1209.) That means two things:

- You must have created a record that shows the error, and
- You must produce enough of the record for the reviewing court to show that the error occurred.

16 **If you fail to produce a meaningful record, the trial court's decision will be affirmed.**

Failing to present a meaningful record can have disastrous consequences for an appellant. "'A necessary corollary to this rule is that if the record is inadequate for meaningful review, the appellant defaults and the decision of the trial court should be affirmed.'" (*Gee v. American Realty & Construction, Inc.* (2002) 99 Cal. App.4th 1412, 1416.) Error must be affirmatively shown; if it is not, the judgment is not reversible. (*Denham v. Superior Court of Los Angeles County* (1970) 2 Cal.3d 557, 564.)

17 Failing to create a meaningful record can occur in a number of ways.

Failing to create a meaningful record can occur in many ways. You might have a sidebar discussion, which may include a ruling by the court, or an in-chambers conference, that was not reported. You can, and should, insist on the court reporter at any time during the trial. You might withdraw certain jury instructions and fail to make those withdrawn instructions part of the record. You might give the court reporter a break and waive reporting certain aspects of the trial, such as voir dire or closing arguments. Failing to present a meaningful record may be more of a matter of choice. However, presenting a "meaningful" record does not mean including only the items that favor your position. For instance, if you are appealing from a summary judgment, the denial or granting of a post-trial motion, or an anti-SLAPP motion, you should designate all documents that were considered at the hearing. That shows you are fair and credible, and you believe your position is strong enough that you will win on the merits. That doesn't mean intentionally omitting the opposing attorney's filings. While this omission could be cured by a counter-designation or a later motion to augment, it does not reflect an objective presentation of the facts and could harm your credibility. In the worst case scenario, the reviewing court may conclude that it does not have an adequate record to make a determination that an error has occurred.

18 Understand how the appellate court looks at errors below.

No one is perfect. During the course of a day, we make plenty of mistakes, little ones and sometimes big ones. A trial is no different. Attorneys will make mistakes, from objecting on the wrong grounds to asking an obviously ambiguous question. A clerk may make a mistake labeling an exhibit. A bailiff could make a mistake in dealing with the jurors. Your clients may also make mistakes by saying the wrong thing or making grimaces that clearly signal their opinions. And the trial court can make mistakes as it rules on evidence and controls the courtroom. At the appellate level, the reviewing court must analyze what type of mistake it is dealing with and determine whether that mistake is harmless or prejudicial. In trying to categorize a mistake, the court will consider (1) who made the mistake, and (2) the effect of the mistake on the proceedings. Some mistakes will work in your favor, while others can hurt your case.

19 Understand the concept of judicial error.

Judicial error is committed when the court intended the order or judgment it made, even though it was based on an error of law. Since a judicial error may be committed by a judge and a clerical error may (or may not be) committed by a clerk, the type of error may be difficult to determine. In *Rochin v. Pat Johnson Manufacturing Co.* (1998) 67 Cal. App.4th 1228, the court described the differences between the two types of errors:

> "The difference between judicial and clerical error rests not upon the party committing the error, but rather on whether it was the deliberate result of judicial reasoning and determination. The distinction between clerical error and judicial error is whether the error was made in rendering the judgment, or in recording the judgment rendered."

(*Id.* at p. 1238.)

20 Be able to distinguish between the different types of errors.

The type of error will determine the remedy. If a simple clerical error was committed, then a party can make a motion before the same tribunal to correct the error. But the court cannot amend a judgment to modify or materially affect the parties' rights under this inherent power. (*Aspen International Capital Corp. v. Marsch* (1991) 235 Cal.App.3d 1199, 1204.) If such an error occurs, and the judgment has been entered, the trial court cannot correct the error and the parties must look to the appellate courts to do so. "Unless the challenged portion of the judgment was entered inadvertently, it cannot be changed post judgment under the guise of correction of clerical error." (*Tokio Marine & Fire Ins. Corp. v. Western Pacific Roofing Corp.* (1999) 75 Cal.App.4th 110, 117.) Thus, if the court "misconstrued the evidence before it, or misapplied the law applicable to the facts disclosed by the evidence, or was even misled by counsel," the error is not a clerical one and must be corrected by a post-judgment motion or on appeal. (*Id.* at p. 118.)

21 Know how to fix clerical errors.

One might be tempted to say that clerical errors are committed only by clerks of the court, but almost anyone involved in the litigation process can make a clerical error. As a general principle, the trial courts possess the inherent power to correct clerical errors in their records so that the court's orders and judgment conform to the truth of the records but it cannot substantially modify a judgment or materially alter the parties' rights, claiming it was merely correcting a clerical error. (*Rochin v. Pat Johnson Manufacturing Co.* (1998) 67 Cal.App.4th 1228, 1238.) "A court of general jurisdiction has this inherent power to correct clerical error in its records, whether made by the court, clerk or counsel, at anytime [sic] so as to conform its records to the truth." (*Aspen International Capital Corp. v. Marsch* (1991) 235 Cal.App.3d 1199, 1204.)

A clear example of a clerical error occurs when a court clerk fails to perform the ministerial duty of entering a judgment in conformity with the court's decision. But, as noted in *Aspen,* a clerical error can be committed by the court, a clerk, or even counsel. (*Ibid.*) The court further noted that "The term 'clerical error' covers all errors, mistakes, or omissions which are not the result of the exercise of the judicial function. If an error, mistake, or omission is the result of inadvertence, but for which a different judgment would have been rendered, the error is clerical and the judgment may be corrected to correspond with what it would have been but for the inadvertence." (*Ibid.*) If you find that a clerical error has been made, the best place to correct it is the superior court level. When clients ask me about appealing a judgment, I review the case to determine whether there is anything that can be done at the lower level to fix the problem. It is quicker, less expensive, and if the trial court understands that an error has been made, it is more effective than turning to appellate courts for relief.

22 **Determine if the error is harmless.**

Appellate courts will frequently examine issues in terms of harmless versus prejudicial error. We hear these terms tossed around quite a bit. A judicial error committed below must be analyzed to categorize the type of error committed. Needless to say, harmless errors will not affect the outcome on an appeal because the reviewing court reasons that the result would be the same even if the error had not occurred. Obviously, this makes sense . . . since a number of errors will almost certainly occur during the course of a trial – because humans are imperfect – then almost every case would be reversible. This result would not make for an efficient judicial system. Code of Civil Procedure section 475 addresses errors not affecting the parties' substantial rights and mandates that the trial court disregard "any error, improper ruling, instruction, or defect, in the pleadings or proceedings which, in the opinion of said court, does not affect the substantial rights of the parties." This section also provides that there is no presumption an error is prejudicial, thus requiring an appellant to demonstrate how the error was prejudicial, affected the substantial rights of the parties, or changed the outcome of the case.

23 Determine if the error is prejudicial.

The fundamental question you must decide in taking an appeal is whether the legal error is prejudicial. If it is not, you might as well stop what you're doing. If it is, please proceed to "Go." The requirement that an error be prejudicial to justify reversal of a judgment or order finds its source in the California Constitution, article VI, section 13: "No judgment shall be set aside, or new trial granted, in any cause, on the ground of misdirection of the jury, or of the improper admission or rejection of evidence, or for any error as to any matter of pleading, or for any error as to any matter of procedure, unless, after an examination of the entire cause, including the evidence, the court shall be of the opinion that the error complained of has resulted in a miscarriage of justice."

24 You must be able to establish prejudicial error.

Code of Civil Procedure section 475 requires that the complaining party establish a prejudicial error that caused the party to suffer "substantial injury," and "that a different result would have been probable if such error, ruling, instruction, or defect had not occurred or existed." Evidence Code section 353 provides that no verdict or finding shall be set aside, or a judgment or decision reversed, based on the ground of erroneous admission of evidence unless the error resulted in "a miscarriage of justice." (Evid. Code, §§ 353(b), 354.)

25 Determine who bears the burden of proving an error was prejudicial.

Since prejudice is not presumed, according to Code of Civil Procedure section 475(b), the appellant bears the burden of affirmatively demonstrating prejudicial error. Trial attorneys will often tell me about errors that occurred during trial. Some of these errors might not be supported by the record, such as in-chamber or sidebar discussions. Once the error has been found in the record, appellant must take a two-prong approach – establish the error exists and it is prejudicial. On the other hand, respondents will also take a two-prong approach - demonstrate that no error occurred but even if it did, the error is not prejudicial. In *Santina v. General Petroleum Corp.* (1940) 41 Cal.App.2d 74, the court discussed this burden:

> "Where any error is relied on for a reversal it is not sufficient for appellant to point to the error and rest there. Since the appellate court must affirmatively find prejudice such finding must be based either upon the facts found in the record or upon the reasonable inferences to be drawn therefrom. In the face of the constitutional limitation there is no room for the presumption that prejudice results from the fact of error alone. The fact of prejudice is just as essential as the fact of error."

(*Id.* at p. 77.)

As noted in *Paterno v. State of California* (1999) 74 Cal. App.4th 68, the court's duty to examine the entire record arises only after the appellant has fulfilled his or her duty to make an argument establishing prejudice. "Because of the need to consider the particulars of a given case, rather than the type of error, the appellant bears the duty of spelling out in his brief exactly how the error caused a miscarriage of justice." (*Id.* at p. 106.)

26 Test the purported error to determine if it results in a miscarriage of justice.

In *Pool v. City of Oakland* (1986) 42 Cal.3d 1051, the court quoted from *Seaman's Direct Buying Service, Inc. v. Standard Oil Co.* (1984) 36 Cal.3d 752, 770 (overruled on other grounds in *Freeman & Mills, Inc. v. Belcher Oil Co.* (1995) 11 Cal.4th 85): "'[A] 'miscarriage of justice' should be declared only when the court, 'after an examination of the entire cause, including the evidence,' is of the 'opinion' that it is reasonably probable that a result more favorable to the appealing party would have been reached in the absence of the error.' " (*Id.* at p. 1069.) More specific language can be found in cases dealing with the error involved, i.e., jury argument, instruction, exclusion or admission of evidence, etc. The court in *Seaman* also acknowledged, "'The test is 'necessarily [ ] based upon reasonable probabilities rather than upon mere possibilities; otherwise the entire purpose of the constitutional provision would be defeated..'" (*Id.* at p. 770.)

27 Determine if the error is "reversible error per se."

"Reversible error per se" occurs when the error is inherently prejudicial and thus the appellant is not required to demonstrate prejudice. These errors frequently involve constitutional issues, such as where a party is deprived of the right to a fair hearing or a jury trial. "A structural error requires reversal without regard to the strength of the evidence or other circumstances." (*In re Enrique G.* (2006) 140 Cal. App.4th 676, 685.) If such errors are committed, the appellant is almost guaranteed a reversal because the impaired right is so fundamental that prejudice is presumed. It may occur where the court denies the parties the right to a jury trial (*Martin v. County of Los Angeles* (1996) 51 Cal.App.4th 688, 697-698), the denial of a party's right to testify or present evidence (*Kelly v. New West Fed. Sav.* (1996) 49 Cal.App.4th 659, 677), the denial of the right to cross-examine witnesses (*Fremont Indem. Co. v. Workers' Comp. Appeals Bd.* (1984) 153 Cal.App.3d 965, 971), or the trial court's failure to render a statement of decision after a timely request. (*Marriage of Ananeh-Firempong* (1990) 219 Cal.App.3d 272, 282-284.) If an appellant can show that an error is "reversible per se," then the burden falls on the respondent to present an adequate record to demonstrate the error was harmless. If the respondent fails to do so, the appellant can win the appeal just by demonstrating the error occurred. (*Lankster v. Alpha Beta Co.* (1993) 15 Cal. App.4th 678, 683-684.)

28 Ascertain whether the error has been invited.

The doctrine of "invited error" acts as an estoppel against an appellant, who cannot complain about an error that he or she "invited" due to conduct that induces or invites error by the trial court. "The 'doctrine of invited error' is an 'application of the estoppel principle': 'Where a party by his conduct induces the commission of error, he is estopped from asserting it as a ground for reversal' on appeal. . . . At bottom, the doctrine rests on the purpose of the principle, which is to prevent a party from misleading the trial court and then profiting therefrom in the appellate court." (*Norgart v. Upjohn Co.* (1999) 21 Cal.4th 383, 403; *Huffman v. Interstate Brands Corp.* (2004) 121 Cal.App.4th 679, 706 ["the invited error doctrine requires affirmative conduct demonstrating a deliberate tactical choice on the part of the challenging party."] This type of error is, in my opinion, a gift if the opposing side made the error, and a major headache if the party I represent has made the error below. Invited error may raise an issue of attorney malpractice. No attorney wants to see language in an opinion that invited error has occurred, unless it is done by the other side. A question arises as to whether the attorney or the party engaged in conduct that permitted the error, or if the attorney had acted differently, the court might have been made aware of the error and had an opportunity to correct it. Invited error might occur when the appellant complains that the court erred in allowing the introduction of inadmissible evidence during part of the trial, if the record shows the appellant offered the same evidence at another time. Another example of invited error could occur when an appellant contends an instruction should not have been given to the jury, but he or she requested the same instruction that was given or one substantially similar to it. (*Horsemen's Benevolent & Protective Assn. v. Valley Racing Assn.* (1992) 4 Cal. App.4th 1538, 1555.) However, this doctrine does not apply if the attorney merely acquiesces after a judicial determination or ruling, because the attorney is merely "'endeavoring to make the best of a bad situation for which he was not responsible.'" (*Mary M. v. City of Los Angeles* (1991) 54 Cal.3d 202, 213.) If you feel that an error has been committed by the opposing party during trial, do not lose the opportunity to point out that the party may have engaged in conduct that invited the error.

29 Distinguish between judicial error and the trial attorney's strategy.

Clients often complain to me about the behavior of their trial attorneys. The complaints range from not returning phone calls, to not paying attention to their suggestions as to how the attorney should have tried the case. It could be a matter of lack of preparation or bad choices. When does a strategic choice become an error? Usually at the end of the case when the clients have lost and the attorney realizes his or her strategy didn't pay off. Quite often, a client will complain that the trial attorney failed to present crucial evidence or failed to properly question a witness. The client may say that he or she urged the attorney to pursue a certain course of action, but often there is no record of these discussions between attorney and client. While strategic choices may result in errors or misjudgments in how the attorney tried the case, typically they do not result in an appealable issue. I may advise a client that the error they seek to raise is really their attorney's strategic choice, an error which the appellate court will not consider. If the client has chosen someone who is green at trial or decides not to pursue a line of questioning, there is nothing I can do. At the extreme end, the attorney's handling of the case may be malpractice. As stated in *Mesecher v. County of San Diego* (1992) 9 Cal.App.4th 1677:

> "There is nothing shocking about these rules [concerning invited error]. They are consistent with the adversary system's appreciation that lawyers in civil litigation must be given adequate breathing room to select whatever trial strategies they deem appropriate. Absent the need for the same constitutional protections afforded to defendants in criminal cases, there is considerable judicial deference to attorney creativity in civil cases. Admittedly the results of such creativity can be mixed with the lawyer and his or her client being rewarded in some cases and not in others. Nonetheless our adversary system requires that we allow counsel the right to maximize the use of his or her trial skills so that the fairness of the result will not be questioned because the court curtailed the lawyer's role.
>
> "Although this laissez faire judicial attitude towards the trial lawyer increases the probability that the outcome in most cases is correct, it also involves the risk that the lawyer's gamble may go awry with a skewed or ambiguous result. Absent unusual circumstances in spite of this risk, appellate courts generally are unwilling to second guess the tactical choices made by counsel during trial. Thus where a deliberate trial strategy results in an outcome disappointing to the advocate, the lawyer may not use that tactical decision as the basis to claim prejudicial error."

(*Id.* at p. 1686.)

30 Attorney malpractice is not a ground for appeal.

Some of these errors, such as prejudicial error or error that is reversible per se, strengthen an appeal. Others, such as harmless or invited error, can ruin the chances for a successful appeal. It isn't uncommon for the client to wonder why he or she lost at trial, especially when so much of the trial is difficult for a layperson to comprehend. There are times when the client will ask about an appeal but the real remedy is an action for attorney malpractice. For instance, if the trial court dismisses a case because the plaintiff has blown the statute of limitations, the judge's order was proper and the error may be due to an attorney's negligence. Other errors are not so obvious to a client. For example, the attorney may have failed to preserve the record by not making a proper objection or an adequate offer of proof. If the attorney has committed these errors, especially failing to raise matters below, then the client's remedy is beyond the reach of an appeal. As an appellate attorney, I often receive case referrals from trial attorneys. Of course, I want to honor these valuable associations but the duty to the client transcends these relationships. Quite often, the relationship between the client and the attorney is already fractured, and the client may even suspect attorney malpractice. I have to tell the client that the error is not appealable but there is a potential malpractice claim. In many of those cases, the client has had some warning about the attorney's performance, but for whatever reason, the client hoped the attorney's performance would improve. Perhaps the answer lies in educating the public about what they have a right to expect from an attorney, how to address their complaints about an attorney's performance (or lack of it), and when to end the relationship without prejudicing their rights.

31 Memorize the first rule of appellate procedure: issues generally cannot be raised for the first time on appeal.

One of the major obstacles faced by appellate attorneys, who are usually called into a case at the end of the proceedings, is the limitation on raising new theories at the appellate stage. As a general rule, an appellant cannot assert a new theory for the first time on appeal. This rule is based on fairness and incorporates principles of estoppel and waiver. Of course, such a rule has profound implications for appellants and their trial attorneys. Having stated the general rule, I want to note there are exceptions. In *Brown v. Boren* (1999) 74 Cal.App.4th 1303, the court stated:

> "It is a firmly entrenched principle of appellate practice that litigants must adhere to the theory on which a case was tried. Stated otherwise, a litigant may not change his or her position on appeal and assert a new theory. To permit this change in strategy would be unfair to the trial court and the opposing litigant . . . To be sure, we have discretion to consider a new theory on appeal when it is purely a matter of applying the law to undisputed facts."

(*Id.* at p. 1316; citations omitted.) *Mattco Forge, Inc. v. Arthur Young & Co.* (1997) 52 Cal. App.4th 820 goes one step further, stating, "Only when the issue presented involves purely a legal question, on an *uncontroverted record and requires no factual determinations,* is it appropriate to address new theories." (*Id.* at p. 847; italics in original.) This situation may occur where everyone agrees on the facts that are relevant to the new issue. The appellate court may also exercise its discretion and consider constitutional issues raised for the first time on appeal "especially when . . . the asserted error fundamentally affects the validity of the judgment . . . or important issues of public policy are at issue . . ." (*County of Orange v. Ivansco* (1998) 67 Cal.

App.4th 328, 331, fn. 2.) For example, public policy concerns arise where cases are disposed of without a trial on the merits or the appellant argues that a local ordinance or state law conflicts with federal law, especially on a constitutional issue.

32 The trial court can be wrong and still be right.

Now contrast this general rule with the principle that the appellate court may affirm a judgment or order if it is correct on *any* theory, regardless of the trial court's expressed reasons. As commonly stated, the appellate court examines the judgment and not the rationale. The result is that the appellate court, and even the respondent, can raise new issues, unless the appellant would be prejudiced, such as the situation where the new theory involves an issue of fact. "The parties' failure to raise the issue in their original appellate briefs does not bar our consideration of it if the parties have had a fair opportunity to present their positions." (*Woodward Park Homeowners Association v. City of Fresno* (2007) 150 Cal.App.4th 683, 714.) Other situations come to mind, such as arguing on appeal how a pleading can be amended after a demurrer is sustained or how a change in law that would have validated the new theory had the law been in existence when the case was tried. The lesson is that the prohibition against raising new issues is not absolute but the trial attorney should make every attempt to present the appellate court with a complete record, rather than hoping for an exception.

~ Tips for Success ~

- Don't rely solely on an appeal to save your case; think about motions and maneuvers that might get you what you want without an appeal.

- Fix clerical errors by making a motion to the trial court.

- The reviewing court will want to preserve a judgment or order as correct; it is your burden to show otherwise.

- Take a two-step approach in analyzing errors: (1) what type of error occurred, and (2) is it prejudicial?

- Produce a meaningful record for the reviewing court that clearly shows judicial error below.

- Be prepared to show the error was prejudicial.

- Examine your conduct and be sure you have not done anything to invite the trial court's error.

- An unsuccessful trial strategy or even legal malpractice - by you or your opponent - are not grounds for appeal.

- In general, you can't raise issues for the first time on appeal; make sure you have raised them at the trial level.

CHAPTER 3. STANDARDS OF REVIEW

An all too familiar scenario: *The jury has just returned its verdict against your client. You can't believe it! After all, you had more witnesses and a better expert. And it was obvious, at least to you, that the witnesses for the other side bald-faced liars! "This appeal should be easy," you tell your appellate attorney. "Just look at our evidence. We had more witnesses and ours were more credible. And the judge made a number of errors. I have asked the court reporter to prepare a transcript of our witnesses' testimony. I think that is all you will need for the appeal."*

Is the attorney correct?

33 The standard of review is the threshold issue of your appeal.

Some cases have characterized the standard of review as the "threshold issue" in every appeal. In *Clothesrigger, Inc. v. GTE Corp.* (1987) 191 Cal.App.3d 605, the court states, "As in every appellate matter, the threshold issue here is the proper standard of review. The hierarchical process and respective roles of the trial and appellate courts involve more than ceremony. Generally appropriate appellate deference to the trial court will be accomplished by affirming a correct trial court order even though the trial court may have given the wrong reason for its actions." (*Id.* at p. 611.) Other courts have characterized the standard of review as "'the degree of deference given by the reviewing court to the actions or decisions under review.'" (*San Francisco Fire Fighters Local 798 v. City and County of San Francisco* (2006) 38 Cal.4th 653, 667.) The standard of review provides the focus of a brief. While the appropriate standard of review may also be an issue in the case, recognition of the standard should guide the attorney's statement of facts and argument so as to satisfy the applicable standard.

34 Recognize the importance of the standards of review on appeal.

Just trying a case is trying enough. How can a trial attorney be expected to look beyond the immediacy of trial and anticipate what a justice (let alone three of them) may need for an appeal that may never be filed? It's understandable that an attorney may want to focus on winning at trial, but the trial attorney is the only person who is in a position to protect the case if an appeal is required. When preparing a case for trial, the attorney must be mindful of who has the burden of proof on certain issues. The next question is whether that burden is satisfied by a preponderance of the evidence or clear and convincing evidence. A standard of review indicates how the reviewing court looks at a purported error. Standards of review only come into the picture after the trial, when there is something to review. No wonder trial attorneys pay little attention to the appropriate standard of review. An issue may also involve a mixture of the standards. Knowing the standard of review is important to the trial attorney so that if an error occurs, the trial attorney understands how to protect the record and present the appellate court with all the information it needs to conduct a meaningful review.

35 **Learn to distinguish among the standards of review.**

Errors are reviewed under three general standards of review, and some standards hold more promise for success on appeal than others. Statistics exist that show how successful certain challenges are. As an appellate practitioner, I am more optimistic about legal errors and independent review than an appeal based on abuse of discretion or lack of substantial evidence. I am also more optimistic about appeals from cases that are terminated early by a demurrer without leave to amend or a motion for summary judgment, both of which are generally reviewed de novo (although abuse of discretion may come into play in the areas of continuances and amendments).

36 **Identify the applicable standard of review in your documents.**

Some appellate briefs fail to even identify the standard of review; they merely argue the trial court erred. Big mistake. You might think that the appellate courts have reviewed thousands of briefs and should know what standard of review to apply, but this is not as easy as it sounds. The parties and the courts can disagree among themselves about which standard applies; the standard can be hotly disputed. The appellant's brief should always identify the standard of review as to each issue while the respondent should note the correct standard if there is a dispute. In *People v. Jackson* (2005) 128 Cal.App.4th 1009, the court stated:

> "However convoluted the facts, or complex the issues, the standard of review is the compass that guides the appellate court to its decision. It defines and limits the course the court follows in arriving at its destination. Deviations from the path, whether it be one most or least traveled, leave writer and reader lost in the wilderness."

(*Id.* at p. 1018.)

37 Ascertain if an independent (or "de novo") standard of review will be applied to review the claimed error.

This standard is applied when the issue is one of law and its resolution does not depend on disputed facts. As a result, the appellate court examines the question de novo without giving any deference to the trial court. "That is not to say the appellate court disregards the trial court's rationale for its decision. It often is most helpful and illustrates the important role trial courts play in shaping the law. We are not averse to using all the help we can get." (*People v. Jackson* (2005) 128 Cal. App.4th 1009, 1018.) Appeals based on this standard usually have a better chance for success because the reviewing court does not filter its decision by considering the reasoning of the trial court. That isn't to say the court has no interest in why and how the trial court reached its decision, but it simply isn't bound by what the trial court decided. The usefulness of the trial court's reasoning may be that it acts as a checklist for the reviewing court.

38 Look to the appellate court to determine questions of law.

The appellate court may believe it is in the same, if not better, position to determine questions of law. After all, the appellate court has the benefit of a collective intellect and more resources for conducting lengthy and exhaustive legal research. Because questions of law are not dependent on credibility or a witness's demeanor, there is no need to defer to the trial court's rulings. Moreover, the appellate courts are concerned with maintaining a uniformity of decision and providing guidance to litigants in other cases, concerns shared by trial courts. Independent review can be applied in resolving constitutional issues, interpretation of statutes, regulations and the rules of court, and legislative validity. The court of appeal will also independently interpret written instruments, unless the parties present conflicting evidence at trial. The application of law to undisputed facts is subject to the appellate court's de novo review. For instance, if the parties stipulate to facts, which then become undisputed, the correct application of law to those facts is subject to independent review. As a result, questions of fact can be transformed into questions of law when the facts are uncontroverted and only one deduction or deduction can reasonably be drawn from those facts. (*Fagerquist v. Western Sun Aviation, Inc.* (1987) 191 Cal. App.3d 709, 719.)

In *Crocker National Bank v. City and County of San Francisco* (1989) 49 Cal.3d 881, the court explained how appellate courts review mixed questions of law and fact:

> "Questions of fact concern the establishment of historical or physical facts; their resolution is reviewed under the substantial-evidence test. Questions of law relate to the selection of a rule; their resolution is reviewed independently. Mixed questions of law and fact concern the application of the rule to the facts and the consequent determination whether the rule

> is satisfied. If the pertinent inquiry requires application of experience with human affairs, the question is predominantly factual and its determination is reviewed under the substantial-evidence test. If, by contrast, the inquiry requires a critical consideration, in a factual context, of legal principles and their underlying values, the question is predominantly legal and its determination is reviewed independently."

(*Id.* at p. 888.) Seems simple enough, huh? You might think so but attorneys squabble quite a bit over this distinction. They even argue over whether certain facts are undisputed, and to what extent. Oh, if I had a nickel for every time an opposing attorney insisted the facts were "undisputed," I might be rich (except for the 40% loss in value of my invested nickels due to the current economy).

39 Know when the abuse of discretion standard of review is applied.

In an appeal based on this standard, the appellate court examines the trial court's discretionary rulings "and asks whether it exceeds the bounds of reason or is arbitrary, whimsical or capricious. . . This standard involves abundant deference to the trial court's rulings." (*People v. Jackson* (2005) 128 Cal.App.4th 1009, 1018; citations omitted.) If you believe the trial court is acting beyond the bounds of reason or is arbitrary, whimsical or capricious, you must try to get that language on the record. Sometimes trial courts are forthcoming about their reasons for ruling in a certain way, other times they prefer to keep it a mystery.

40 Yes, you can win an appeal based on abuse of discretion by the trial court.

An appellant challenging a discretionary ruling on this ground will have the best chance of success if he or she can demonstrate the trial court failed to adhere to legal criteria. This showing makes the ruling a clear case of abuse and a miscarriage of justice. If you are hoping to find that the trial court acted "beyond the bounds of reason," think again. While you may not like the court's ruling, finding a judge who is irrational and acts beyond reason is not that easy, although such a judge can be found in Hollywood movies. Consider the explanation of this standard of review in *Horsford v. Board of Trustees of State California University* (2005) 132 Cal.App.4th 359, 393:

> "This description of the standard is complete, however, only if 'beyond the bounds of reason' is understood as something in addition to simply 'irrational' or 'illogical.' While an irrational decision would usually constitute an abuse of discretion, the legal standard of review encompasses more than that: 'The scope of discretion always resides in the particular law being applied, i.e., in the 'legal principles governing the subject of [the] action . . .' Action that transgresses the confines of the applicable principles of law is outside the scope of discretion and we call such action an 'abuse' of discretion.' . . . For example, a court could be mistaken about the scope of its discretion and the mistake could be entirely 'reasonable' – that is, it adopts a position about which reasonable judges could differ. But a reasoned decision based on the reasonable view of the scope of discretion is still an abuse of judicial discretion when it starts from a mistaken premise, even though nothing about the

> exercise of discretion is, in ordinary-language use of the phrase, 'beyond the bounds of reason.' . . . In other words, judicial discretion must be measured against the general rules of law and, in the case of a statutory grant of discretion, against the specific law that grants the discretion."

(*Id.* at p. 393; citations omitted.) "'A trial court's exercise of discretion will be upheld if it is based on a 'reasoned judgment' and complies with the ' . . . legal principles and policies appropriate to the particular matter at issue.'" (*Color-Vue, Inc. v. Abrams* (1996) 44 Cal. App.4th 1599, 1603.) Simply put, "A trial court abuses its discretion when it applies the wrong legal standards applicable to the issue at hand." (*Adams v. Aerojet-General Corp.* (2001) 86 Cal. App.4th 1324, 1341, citing from *Paterno v. State of California* (1999) 74 Cal.App.4th 68, 85.)

41 **Accept that reversals based on abuse of discretion are rare.**

The appellate courts give considerable deference to the trial court in making discretionary rulings, especially when there are several permissible options available to the lower court. This standard of review also presents a tough challenge on appeal, but as noted above, the chances of success are increased when the ruling goes outside applicable principles of law and results in a miscarriage of justice. At the trial level, the attorney must show how the court's ruling conflicts with those principles of law, and also, how the ruling will result in prejudicial error. In *Estate of Gilkison* (1998) 65 Cal. App.4th 1443, the court described a challenge based on abuse of discretion:

> "An attorney who prosecutes an appeal from an order addressed to the trial court's sound discretion is confronted with more than a daunting

> task. This is an uphill battle which, absent unusual circumstances, may be equated with confederate General John Bell Hood's attempt to capture 'Little Round Top' at the battle of Gettysburg in the Civil War. General Hood did not succeed."

(*Id.* at p. 1448.)

42 Consider the disadvantages inherent in an appeal based on lack of substantial evidence.

The substantial evidence standard of review applies where the order or judgment involves the trial court's determination of disputed fact issues. It is frequently raised when a trial has been concluded and the jury or court found in favor of one party over the other based on the evidence presented. This ground may also arise when the trial court or jury resolves any factual dispute. Simply stated, the appellate courts are bound by the trial court's resolution of disputed factual issues and must affirm the judgment so long as the judgment is supported by "substantial evidence." (*Winograd v. American Broadcasting Co.* (1998) 68 Cal.App.4th 624, 632.)

43 In substantial evidence appeals, don't weigh the evidence but look to the evidence supporting the judgment.

Of all the standards of review, this standard is probably the weakest. Reversals are rare, although not impossible, and as noted in *Whiteley v. Philip Morris Inc.* (2004) 117 Cal.App.4th 635, 678, "[d]efendants raising a claim of insufficiency of the evidence assumes [sic] a *daunting burden.*" So, what is considered substantial evidence? "Substantial evidence" must be "of ponderable legal significance. . .

reasonable in nature, credible, and of solid value . . . 'Obviously the word cannot be deemed synonymous with 'any' evidence.'" (*Bowers v. Bernards* (1984) 150 Cal.App.3d 870, 873.) Moreover, in resolving appeals based on this ground, the courts will look to the *entire* record, and not just to evidence that is favorable to the appellant or isolated from a consideration of the record as a whole. (*Ibid.*) In my opinion, the term "substantial evidence" is not accurate. To say that substantial evidence supports the judgment implies a weighing or that the quantity of evidence is somehow significant. We know that is not always the case. Juries are often instructed that they can believe one witness over a multitude of witnesses. What matters is whether there is credible evidence to support the decision.

44 Don't bother directly arguing about credibility in a substantial evidence challenge.

An appeal on this ground should avoid examining the evidence with a focus on credibility, because that is the function of the trier of fact and not the appellate courts. Clients will often complain that a witness has lied, but unless that lie can be affirmatively established on the record, the jury is entitled to believe whom it wants. (*Tupman v. Haberkern* (1929) 208 Cal. 256, 261; *In re Marriage of Ananeh-Firempong* (1990) 219 Cal.App.3d 272, 278.) Nor does it matter that the appellate court, or even the trial court, had they been the trier of fact, might have ruled in another way or even found there was substantial evidence to support a different decision. The appellate court cannot substitute its opinions and conclusions for those of the trier of fact. (*Bowers v. Bernards, supra,* 150 Cal. App.3d 870, 874 ["*If such substantial evidence can be found, it is of no consequence that the trial court believing other evidence, or drawing other reasonable inferences, might have reached a contrary conclusion.*"] (Italics in original.)

45 Challenge a verdict or judgment that is not supported by substantial evidence.

Appealing on this ground is often unsuccessful but that doesn't mean an appellant is always without hope. The attack should not be based on the quantity of evidence but rather the quality of it. As noted in *Kuhn v. Department of General Services* (1994) 22 Cal.App.4th 1627, "While it is commonly stated that our 'power' begins and ends with a determination that there is substantial evidence . . ., this does not mean we must blindly seize any evidence in support of the respondent in order to affirm the judgment. The Court of Appeal 'was not created . . . merely to echo the determinations of the trial court. A decision supported by a mere scintilla of evidence need not be affirmed on review.'" (*Id.* at p. 1633, citations omitted.) *Kuhn* also noted that it is not enough to have "any *evidence* supporting the judgment; it must be "reasonable . . . , credible, and of solid value. . . . The ultimate determination is whether a *reasonable* trier of fact could have found for the respondent based on the *whole* record." *(Id.* at p. 1633.) *Kuhn* included inferences as part of the entire record as does *In re Estate of Young* (2008) 160 Cal. App.4th 62, 76 [court distinguishes between inferences based on "logic and reason," rather than "mere speculation or conjecture."]

46 If you are appealing based on lack of substantial evidence, be prepared to show that the evidence supporting the verdict or judgment is not reasonable.

What this means for the appellant is that if the respondent has prevailed based on evidence that is not reasonable, then the appellant must present facts showing the unreasonableness of the testimony. For instance, if a single witness testified to what he or she observed, then contrary facts showing either the witness could never have observed those facts or wasn't even in the same location must be in the record. This requires a showing that the evidence is "inherently improbable" or "implausible" so that the falsity or impossibility of the evidence is apparent or it is physically impossible that the evidence is true. (*Evje v. City Title Ins. Co.* (1953) 120 Cal. App.2d 488, 492.) Simply rearguing the *weight* of the evidence will not satisfy this standard.

47 Make sure you provide a complete record of the proceedings below if you intend to challenge the sufficiency of the evidence.

If you intend to rely on this standard of review, you must provide a reporter's transcript of the proceedings. If you don't, you will not be able to challenge the sufficiency of the evidence because you won't be able to present the *entire* record to the court. The appellate court will conclusively presume that the evidence supports the judgment. (*In re Estate of Fain* (1999) 75 Cal.App.4th 973, 992.) In *In re Estate of Fain, supra,* the court stated:

> "Where no reporter's transcript has been provided and no error is apparent on the face of the existing appellate record, the judgment must be *conclusively presumed correct* as to *all evidentiary matters.* To put it another way, it is presumed that the unreported trial testimony would demonstrate the absence of error . . . The effect of this rule is that an appellant who attacks a judgment but supplies no reporter's transcript will be precluded from raising an argument as to the sufficiency of the evidence."

(*Id.* at p. 992.) (Italics in original; citation omitted.) It makes sense that the reporter's transcript must be provided, especially when the standard requires a consideration of the *entire* record. (*In re Estate of Young* (2008) 160 Cal.App.4th 62, 76.) Quite often, the losing party will be able to point to favorable evidence – often ignoring the evidence supporting the winning party. Taking this approach can result in alienating the court, particularly when the winning party can present a whole laundry list of evidence that was favorable to him or her. This approach can even result in a waiver of the point on appeal. (*Nwosu v. Uba* (2004) 122 Cal. App.4th 1229, 1246 [appellant must present all material evidence on a point, not merely their own evidence].) As a point of caution, appellants often complain that the evidence in favor of the respondent cannot be substantial because the other side was lying and was simply not credible. That is not enough because the trier of fact can believe one side and not another. But if the evidence is not credible because the testimony was physically impossible or obviously false, then such a challenge might be successful. What is important here is to provide the facts necessary to show *on the record,* and not for the first time on appeal, that the purported evidence is either physically impossible or false.

48 Know when a presumption favors the appellant.

Presumptions that favor the appellant arise most frequently in appeals from a judgment of dismissal after a demurrer is sustained without leave to amend, or after granting a motion for judgment on the pleadings. These types of appeals switch the presumption in favor of the judgment to a presumption that favors the appellant. When such a presumption exists, the appellate court must presume the truth of allegations or evidence favorable to the appellant. In reviewing the case, the appellate court assumes the truth of all facts properly pleaded by the plaintiff. (*Blank v. Kirwan* (1985) 39 Cal.3d 311, 318; *Kempton v. City of Los Angeles* (2008) 165 Cal.App.4th 1344, 1347.) "'We independently review the ruling on a demurrer and determine de novo whether the pleading alleges facts sufficient to state a cause of action. . . We construe the pleading in a reasonable manner and read the allegations in context.'" (*SC Manufactured Homes, Inc. v. Liebert* (2008) 162 Cal.App.4th 68, 82; citations omitted.)

49 Argue the presumption in favor of appellant in summary judgment, nonsuits and directed verdict motions.

A presumption also frequently arises in appeals from a dismissal after an order for summary judgment has been granted. In reviewing the appeal, the appellate court will strictly construe the moving papers and liberally construe the opposing papers. It will also view the moving papers in a light most favorable to the losing appellant. Finally, all doubts about granting the motion are resolved in favor of denial. "'We are not bound by the trial court's stated reasons or rationales . . . 'Summary judgment is a drastic remedy to be used sparingly, and any doubts about the propriety of summary judgment must be resolved in favor of the opposing party.'" (*Kasparian v. AvalonBay Communities, Inc.* (2007) 156 Cal. App.4th 11, 19.) This presumption in favor of the appellant is also applied in nonsuits and directed verdicts, although the substantial evidence standard is applicable in reviewing the appeal. Thus, the court will assume plaintiff's evidence as true, including reasonable inferences, and determine whether the plaintiff has stated a cause of action. (*Freeman v. Lind* (1986) 181 Cal.App.3d 791, 799; *Estate of Fossa* (1962) 210 Cal.App.2d 464, 466.) If a motion *in limine* is construed as "the functional equivalent" of a nonsuit, the applicable standard of review will be the same. (*Fergus v. Songer* (2007) 150 Cal. App.4th 552, 569-570.)

50 Assert that your client is entitled to a presumption in favor of the judgment in challenges based on erroneous or refused jury instructions.

In appeals involving erroneous or refused jury instructions, appellants also enjoy presumptions in their favor. In such cases, the appellate court views the evidence in the light most favorable to the claim of instructional error, assuming the jury might have believed the evidence upon which the instruction was predicated and the jury might have rendered a verdict in appellant's favor. (*Whiteley v. Philip Morris, Inc.* (2004) 117 Cal.App.4th 635, 655; *Ayala v. Arroyo Vista Family Health Center* (2008) 160 Cal.App.4th 1350, 1358.)

51 Argue that the evidence presented by plaintiffs in appeals from anti-SLAPP motions is entitled to a presumption in favor of the judgment.

While reviews of anti-SLAPP motions are done on an independent standard, the appellate court will presume and accept as true appellant's evidence and consider the respondent's evidence only to determine if it has defeated the appellant's evidence as a matter of law. "We review the trial court's order de novo . . . We will not weigh the evidence; rather, we accept as true evidence favorable to the plaintiff, and evaluate evidence favorable to the defendant to determine whether it defeats the plaintiff's claim as a matter of law." (*Neville v. Chudacoff* (2008) 160 Cal.App.4th 1255, 1262; citations omitted.)

~ Tips for Success ~

- Know your standards of review; it is the threshold issue that determines how the appellate court will review the appeal.

- Determining which standard of review applies will help you identify what part of the transcripts you need to create a meaningful record for the appellate court.

- Look for legal errors, such as a violation, misinterpretation, or misapplication of law, to strengthen your appeal.

- Don't bother with arguments based on credibility or the weight of evidence; the appellate court will not decide factual disputes.

- Carefully consider going forward with an appeal based solely on the lack of substantial evidence to support the verdict; they are very difficult to win.

CHAPTER 4. IT ALL BEGINS WITH AN OBJECTION

An all too familiar scenario: *Even though you've just lost your case, you are sure the jury did not have a full understanding of the facts because the judge refused to admit some of your evidence and allowed confusing testimony from the opposing side's witnesses. You call your appellate attorney and start to list the judge's adverse rulings.*

The appellate attorney asks, "Did you object to the admission of the evidence?"

"Well, of course, I did," you respond. "Okay, I am pretty sure I did. There was so much going on, it's hard to remember, but I know I said something."

"Did you get a ruling on your objections?"

You are silent for a moment as you try to recall what happened. "I tried, but you know, we were all talking and I think the judge may have forgotten to rule."

The appellate attorney asks if you made an offer of proof on testimony that the judge had ruled was inadmissible. Now you're really exasperated!

"What was the point?" you ask. "It was obvious that the judge was not going to let in the evidence!"

What should the attorney have done to protect the record?

52 Know how to object.

The importance of objections in preserving the record on appeal cannot be emphasized enough. To me, it is as important as saying "I do" during a wedding ceremony. Until you speak those two little words, the wedding cannot be completed. In a similar vein, until you object, you have not preserved the issue on appeal. Challenging the admission of evidence generally takes three forms, depending on the timing:

1. A pre-emptive motion *in limine* before trial begins;
2. An immediate objection at the time the evidence is to come in; and
3. A motion to strike if a witness answers before you can object or before the judge can rule on your objection, or the response is non-responsive.

The biggest problem I have observed in this area is that the trial attorney fails to make a proper objection on the ground to which an appeal is being taken or the judge fails to rule on the objection. These problems can arise when an objection is made - the opposing party and court engage in a discussion, and the attorney who objected loses sight of the fact that a ruling has not been made. Whether this omission can be cured by simply asking the court for a ruling may depend upon the passage of time between the objection and the request. All too often, the omission is forgotten and the trial moves forward.

53 Make written objections in motions for summary judgment.

In motions for summary judgment, the objecting party must either (1) submit objections in writing pursuant to California Rules of Court, rule 3.1354 or (2) make arrangements for a court reporter to be present at the hearing. (Cal. Rules of Court, rule 3.1352.) I always recommend preparing written objections. Written objections must be served and filed at the same time as the objecting party's opposition or reply papers are due. (Cal. Rules of Court, rule 3.1354(a).) You want the judge to have the benefit of your written objections while he or she is reviewing the motion. You don't want the judge to engage in a comprehensive review, reach a tentative decision, and then hear objections *for the first time* at the hearing. If, for some reason, you are forced to wait until the hearing, then I would recommend that your objections be as specific as required of written objections in California Rules of Court, rule 3.1354(b). (See Strategic Tool, No. 92.)

54 Include a proposed order with your written objections in motions for summary judgment.

Pursuant to California Rules of Court, rule 3.1354(c), you must also provide a proposed order to allow the court to rule on written objections. What could be easier? The court simply has to check the lines for "sustained" or "overruled." And if you forget to ask the court for a ruling, you have a document in your hand to remind you. Despite this seemingly streamlined procedure, I still recommend that the objecting attorney limit his or her objections to those that are truly important to the motion as no judge wants to rule on numerous objections, especially when they relate to unimportant facts or the objections are boilerplate. Presenting the trial court with a select few objections enhances the chances of getting a ruling. (See Strategic Tool, No. 92.)

55 Relying on oral objections in motions for summary judgment can be risky.

Relying on an oral objection poses a risk that you might forget to obtain a ruling. A similar problem might arise where the objecting party fails to prepare a proposed order, which is mandatory under California Rules of Court, rule 3.1354(c).) If you know the objection in advance and just forgot - yikes! - to prepare written objections, you might consider preparing a proposed order in a the format required under rule 3.1354(c) to accompany your oral objection.

56 Become familiar with *Biljac Associates v. First Interstate Bank.*

What about the judge who refuses to rule on your objections even though you request a ruling, or says that he or she will only consider admissible evidence? This situation may arise when the judge forgets to rule on the objection or states something like "the court will only consider admissible evidence" or it is "following *Biljac* and is only considering the relevant and pertinent evidence." Of course, it makes sense that the trial court would only consider admissible evidence, but you - and the appellate court - may not be able to tell from the record what the trial court considered admissible and inadmissible. When the trial court refers to *Biljac,* it means *Biljac Associates v. First Interstate Bank* (1990) 218 Cal.App.3d 1410, a controversial case in which the appellate court held that a trial court is not required to issue formal rulings on objections because a summary judgment will be upheld if it is correct on any grounds, even those not relied on by the trial court. In addition, the court in *Biljac* raised a presumption that a trial court is not relying on irrelevant or incompetent evidence when it makes its ruling.

Bijac has also been repeatedly criticized by many courts of appeal; even the same court that decided it later disapproved the *Biljac* procedure in *Demps v. San Francisco Housing Authority* (2007) 149

Cal.App.4th 564, 566. In the recent case of *Reid v. Google, Inc.* (2010) 50 Cal.4th 512, the California Supreme Court extensively discussed *Biljac* and disapproved of it "to the extent it permits the trial court to avoid ruling on specific evidentiary objections." (*Id.* at pg. 532, fn. 8.) Despite the decision in *Reid v. Google, supra,* one might expect some trial courts continue to rely on it to avoid making a ruling on objections, especially when there are numerous objections; and therefore, trial attorneys should be familiar with this case.

57 Don't go overboard in making objections in motions for summary judgment.

If you have complied with California Rules of Court, rule 3.1354(c) (and kept your objections down to a sensible number), then the judge will have a printed order with a space to make those rulings. It should be harder for the trial court to overlook that duty or forget it during the hearing. Certainly you don't want to waive the objection but neither do you want to annoy the judge by making repeated requests for a ruling. How many requests are enough? Well, I wouldn't stop at one. A request should be made when the objections are discussed, and if nothing happens, at the conclusion of the hearing. If the trial court refuses to rule, you want that refusal on the record. The California Supreme Court's recent decision in *Reid v. Google* (2010) 50 Cal.4th 512 should be helpful in this regard, and eliminate the need to keep pestering the trial court for a ruling, by holding that making the objection is enough to preserve the ground for appeal.

58 Recognize that objections are important at both the trial and appellate court levels.

Objections are important on two levels, during trial and when the case is on appeal. At trial, the attorney is concerned with having some control over the flow of the trial, and especially, the testimony and other evidence. Generally, the goal is to keep out certain evidence or restrict the evidence presented by the opposing side. A proper objection must satisfy the procedural rules of the Code of Civil Procedure and the Evidence Code. No one likes to lose a good ground for appeal by failing to say a few magical words.

59 Focus on correcting the error at the trial court level.

At the appellate level, an objection is necessary to show that the objector did everything possible to correct the error by alerting the court and opposing counsel of the problem. Such an objection, if sustained, would have the effect of correcting the problem, while an overruled objection may not help at the trial level but at least will protect the record on appeal. To preserve an issue for appeal, the appellant must raise the objection below before the trial court. "'"The party also must cite to the record showing exactly where the objection was made."'" (*K.C. Multimedia, Inc. v. Bank of America Technology & Operations, Inc.* (2009) 171 Cal.App.4th 939, 948.) "[A] reviewing court ordinarily will not consider a challenge to a ruling if an objection could have been but was not made in the trial court...The purpose of this rule is to encourage parties to bring errors to the attention of the trial court, so that they may be corrected." (*In re S.B.* (2004) 32 Cal.4th 1287, 1293; citation omitted.)

60 Don't lose your appeal by failing to object.

The failure to object and to take all steps necessary to properly follow through with an objection has serious consequences on appeal. It means that the error is waived and cannot be challenged on appeal. "In light of this section [Evidence Code section 353], questions relating to the admissibility of evidence will not be reviewed on appeal in the absence of a specific and timely objection." (*Leonardini v. Shell Oil Co.* (1989) 216 Cal.App.3d 547, 584.) The courts have made exceptions where the record shows that continued objections would be an idle act or the court refuses to rule on the objections, but you must still make a diligent effort to obtain a ruling. (*City of Long Beach v. Farmers & Merchants Bank of Long Beach* (2000) 81 Cal. App.4th 780, 784-785, overruled on other grounds in *Reid v. Google* (2010) 50 Cal.4th 512.) "It is well settled by statute and case authority that the failure to object, even to otherwise inadmissible evidence, waives the defect." (*Haskell v. Carli* (1987) 195 Cal.App.3d 124, 129; Evidence Code section 353(a).) Interposing objections requires an attorney to be quick on his or her feet. After all, it does little good for the trial attorney to ponder whether a question is objectionable, waiting before making it until seven questions later. The objection may be untimely, and worse yet, it may be impossible to undo the damage of the jury having heard the evidence.

61 Memorize the rules for making a proper objection.

The components of a proper objection are outlined in Evidence Code section 353: (1) it must be timely made, and (2) the specific ground of the objection must be included. "Section 353 does not specify the form in which an objection must be made; hence, the use of a continuing objection to a line of questioning would be proper under Section 353 just as it is under existing law." (See Comment by

Assembly Committee on Judiciary to Evidence Code section 353.) Typically, the attorney would use the word "objection" followed by the specific ground. Attorneys often make objections that consist of "Objection" and "I object," without the grounds stated, especially where the grounds may seem very obvious to all. The better practice is to always indicate the grounds even if they seem obvious or are part of a continuing objection.

62 **Be sure to state the grounds for an objection.**

At a minimum, the attorney must state the grounds for an objection. (Evid. Code, § 353(a).) "Evidence Code section 353 does not exalt form over substance. No particular form of objection or motion is required; it is sufficient that the presentation contains a request to exclude specific evidence on the specific legal ground urged on appeal." (*People v. Morris* (1991) 53 Cal.3d 152, 188, disapproved on other grounds in *People v. Stansbury* (1995) 9 Cal.4th 824, 830, fn. 1.) Making an objection on the wrong ground will not help you on appeal. It is not enough that you made a general objection without a ground or objected on a different ground. If you object on one ground, that will not preserve the objection on another ground. (*People v. Holt* (1997) 15 Cal.4th 619, 666, modified at 15 Cal.4th 1385a; *Platzer v. Mammoth Mountain Ski Area* (2002) 104 Cal.App.4th 1253, 1260-1261.) Nor should you rely on a "continuing objection" to preserve the error. Be clear in making a specific objection to the evidence and possibly renew the objection when the questioning exceeds the scope of your original objection or too much time has passed since the original objection.

63 Be careful in relying on continuing objections.

What do you do in the event you want to object to a line of questions? A "continuing" objection to certain evidence or a line of questioning may not be necessary after each question, but your objection should be based on the same ground. (*Smith v. County of Los Angeles* (1989) 214 Cal.App.3d 266, 285.) Be careful if the later questions are different in nature, especially where they cover different subject matter and are objectionable on different grounds. (*Boeken v. Philip Morris Inc.* (2005) 127 Cal.App.4th 1640, 1676 [objection should relate to "a particular, identifiable body of evidence"].) If you have another objection on different grounds, you should state the objection, specifically identifying the new grounds. While the Supreme Court has indicated that the rule that objections not made are forfeited is not automatic, it also noted "the appellate court's discretion to excuse forfeiture should be exercised rarely and only in cases presenting an important legal issue." (*In re S.B.* (2004) 32 Cal.4th 1287, 1293.) That means you should not simply rely on a continuing objection, and if you can show some special circumstances, this rule of forfeiture may not be applied in your case.

64 Know when to make a motion to strike.

Evidence Code section 353 prohibits setting aside a verdict or finding, or reversing a judgment due to the erroneous admission of evidence without an objection or a motion to exclude or strike on the record. (Evid. Code, § 353(a).) An objection is typically used if the evidence has not come in, while a motion to strike is used if the witness testifies before the attorney can object or before the trial court has an opportunity to rule on the objection. By then, although the jury may have heard the evidence, the ground can be preserved for a later challenge on appeal.

65 Know when to use a motion *in limine.*

If you are aware that the opposing party will seek to introduce certain damaging evidence, then you may want to use a motion *in limine*, which allows for a more in-depth discussion about the evidence and the law related to its admission or exclusion than an objection raised at trial. "The advantage of such motions is to avoid the obviously futile attempt to 'unring the bell' in the event a motion to strike is granted in the proceedings before the jury." (*Hyatt v. Sierra Boat Co.* (1978) 79 Cal.App.3d 325, 337.) Motions *in limine* can streamline trials so that the process is not bogged down with objections, sidebar or in-chambers conferences, or hearings out of the presence of the jury, which might be milling around outside, frustrated by a delay that they know nothing about. A ruling on a motion *in limine* may enhance the flow of evidence during trial, and quite possibly, promote settlement. (*Kelly v. New West Federal Savings* (1996) 49 Cal.App.4th 659, 670.)

66 Don't overload the trial court with voluminous motions *in limine.*

Quite often, trial judges complain about counsel who submit a voluminous amount of motions *in limine*, particularly when the goal is to exclude *any* unfavorable evidence and prevent the jury from weighing all of the evidence. In *Pellegrini v. Weiss* (2008) 165 Cal. App.4th 515, the court explained:

> "Generally speaking, in limine motions are disfavored in cases in which they are used not to determine in advance the court's projected ruling if presented with an evidentiary objection during trial, but instead to serve as a substitute for a dispositive statutory motion. The increasing prevalence of

> the practice of using in limine motions in this way produces substantial risk of reversal, particularly in situations in which the constitutional rights to jury trial and confrontation are implicated. As we stated in the recent case of *Amtower v. Photon Dynamics, Inc.* (2008) 158 Cal.App.4th 1582, 1594, 71 Cal.Rptr.3d 361: 'The disadvantages of such shortcuts are obvious. They circumvent procedural protections provided by the statutory motions or by trial on the merits; they risk blindsiding the nonmoving party; and, in some cases, they could infringe [on] a litigant's right to a jury trial. (Cal. Const., art. I, § 16.)' . . . 'The better practice in nearly every case is to afford the litigant the protections provided by trial or by the statutory processes.'"

(*Id.* at p. 530; citation omitted.) Under these circumstances, the trial court will simply defer a decision on the motion until the issue comes up during trial, at which time it can deal with the objection. Trial judges tend to become a bit persnickety when faced with a huge pile of motions *in limine*, particularly if the motions are clearly boilerplate, form motions. They also see such motions as an attempt to keep out everything unfavorable to the moving party, burying the other side in paper, and creating more opportunities for "billable events."

In *Kelly v. New West Federal Savings* (1996) 49 Cal.App.4th 659, a case frequently cited by judges and attorneys at seminars on motions *in limine,* the court acknowledged their advantages but also discussed the following improper uses of such motions:

- Excluding testimony that is speculative, especially when the moving party fails to identify the particular testimony.
- Excluding testimony of prior incidents unless an appropriate foundation is established to show relevance or that the prior incidents were similar in

nature to the subject incident. Without knowing the facts of each incident, the trial court would be required to rule in a vacuum.

- Excluding opinions beyond those expressed at deposition or in written reports, but the moving party fails to identify those opinions.
- Preventing a party from calling witnesses not previously identified in discovery responses, but without any belief that this might occur.
- Excluding evidence that must be heard in context at trial so the court can ascertain its probative value and potential for prejudice.
- Covers matters of day-to-day trial logistics and common professional courtesy.
- Pertains to procedural matters and items related to jury selection.
- Sets forth restatements of current law, such as not referring to the existence of insurance.
- Requires a witness or party to conform trial testimony to a preconceived factual scenario based on testimony given during pretrial discovery.
- Seeks to exclude evidence as a sanction, including issue preclusion, for abuse of the discovery process or presents situations involving waiver or estoppel.
- Requests exclusion of evidence based on an objection under Evidence Code section 352, which requires the trial court to exercise its discretion reasonably according to the facts before the court.
- Attempts to prohibit a party from changing his or her story told during litigation, and according to the moving party, would amount to "surprise," which can be minimized by pretrial discovery and conferences or dealt with in a request for a continuance of the trial or post-trial motions.

- Seeks to exclude expert testimony without notice or adequate warning that a party will be left without an expert.
- Requests exclusion of evidence that is prejudicial to a party, especially if it is relevant to the primary issues of the case, and goes to credibility or the weight of the evidence. If the trial court improperly grants a motion on this ground, it may result in the denial of a fair hearing and "[d]enying a party the right to testify or to offer evidence is reversible per se." (*Id.* at p. 677.)

Attorneys would do well to avoid trying their cases by a motion *in limine*, and should file only those that are critical to the case. Tailor the motion *in limine* to the case and avoid the boilerplate. By doing so, you will be enhancing your credibility and quite possibly, your chances of winning the motion. Finally, consider other methods to attack unfavorable evidence during trial.

67 After a motion *in limine* is denied and evidence is deemed admissible, make an objection when the evidence is actually offered.

Generally when the court has made a ruling on a motion *in limine* that the evidence is admissible, the party seeking exclusion must object when the evidence is actually offered to preserve the issue for appeal. "The reason for this rule is that until the evidence is actually offered, and the court is aware of its relevance in context, its probative value, and its potential for prejudice, matters related to the state of the evidence at the time an objection is made, the court cannot intelligently rule on admissibility. When the parties stipulate on the record, as they did here, that a ruling on an *in limine* motion to exclude evidence will be binding, that stipulation should be deemed a continuing objection to admission. Failure to renew the objection when the evidence is offered does not waive the right to assert error on appeal in these circumstances." (*People v. Jennings* (1988) 46 Cal.3d 963, 975, fn. 3.) As noted in *Summers v. A.L. Gilbert Co.* (1999) 69 Cal. App.4th 1155, "A motion *in limine* to exclude evidence is normally sufficient to preserve an issue for review without the necessity for defendant to renew an objection at the time the evidence was offered . . . However, if the evidence presented during trial is substantially different from that presented at the hearing on the motion *in limine* or included in an offer of proof, it is incumbent on the party who made the motion to renew the objection to the evidence." (*Id.* at p. 1184; citations omitted.)

68 Don't forget to make an offer of proof if the trial court is inclined to exclude your evidence.

When you are trying to admit evidence during trial that the other side wants to exclude, and the trial court is leaning or has ruled in favor of exclusion, then you have to respond with an offer of proof. You need to let the trial and appellate courts know what the evidence might reveal and how important it is to your case. The offer of proof shows what the evidence would have been, who the witness is, and to what issue it is relevant. "Normally the exclusion of evidence will not be considered on appeal unless the substance, purpose and relevance of the excluded evidence was made known to the trial court," or unless the court has clearly stated it is excluding an entire area of evidence. (*Pacific Gas & Electric Co. v. Zuckerman* (1987) 189 Cal.App.3d 1113, 1142; Evidence Code § 354 [the offer of proof should include "the substance, purpose, and relevance of the excluded evidence . . ."].) "Merely setting forth the substance of facts to be proved does not constitute compliance with Evidence Code section 354, subdivision (a)." (*Semsch v. Henry Mayo Newhall Memorial Hospital* (1985) 171 Cal.App.3d 162, 168

[The offer of proof should include the specific testimony to be elicited, its purpose, and the person giving the testimony].) A judgment cannot be set aside on this ground unless "the substance, purpose and relevance of the excluded evidence were made known to the court by an offer of proof or by other means (Evid. Code, § 354, subd. (a).)" (*Gordon v. Nissan Motor Co., Ltd.* (2009) 170 Cal. App.4th 1103, 1113.) However, if an entire class of evidence has been declared inadmissible, or the trial court has indicated it will not receive evidence on a particular issue, then an offer of proof is not a prerequisite to raising the question on appeal, and the offer, if made by counsel, may be "broad and general." (*Pacific Gas & Electric Co. v. Zuckerman, supra,* at p. 1142.)

69 Make an offer of proof if the trial court grants a motion *in limine.*

Don't forget to make an offer of proof if the trial court grants your opponent's motion *in limine.* Your offer of proof may be included in your written opposition to the moving party's motion. (Evid. Code, § 354.)

70 Certain orders or rulings are deemed excepted to without a formal objection.

Code of Civil Procedure section 647 provides "All of the following are deemed excepted to: the verdict of the jury; the final decision in an action or proceeding; an interlocutory order or decision, finally determining the rights of the parties, or some of them; an order or decision from which an appeal may be taken; an order sustaining or overruling a demurrer, allowing or refusing to allow an amendment to a pleading, striking out or refusing to strike out a pleading or a portion thereof, or refusing a continuance; an order made upon ex parte application, giving an instruction, refusing to give an instruction, or modifying an instruction requested; an order or decision made in the absence of the party or an order granting or denying a nonsuit or a motion to strike out evidence or testimony; a ruling sustaining or overruling an objection to evidence; and any statement or other action of the court in commenting upon or in summarizing the evidence. *If the party, at the time when the order, ruling, action or decision is sought or made, or within a reasonable time thereafter, makes known his position thereon, by objection or otherwise, all other orders, rulings, actions or decisions are deemed to have been excepted to."* (Emphasis added.)

71 **Obtain a ruling on your objections.**

You've made your objection but you can't stop there. You must also obtain a ruling on your objections from the trial court. (*City of Long Beach v. Farmers & Merchants Bank of Long Beach* (2000) 81 Cal. App.4th 780, 784, overruled on other grounds in *Reid v. Google* (2010) 50 Cal.4th 512.) It's easy to get lost in discussions with the court and opposing counsel, and quite often under these circumstances, a ruling on an objection will be forgotten. The same advice applies to motions *in limine* and motions to strike. Get a ruling to your objections. If you disagree with the court's ruling, note your objection, otherwise you may have waived any argument that the ruling was incorrect.

~ Tips for Success~

- Know how to make a timely and proper objection.
- State all of the applicable grounds for objection.
- Whenever possible, obtain a ruling on your objection.
- In motions for summary judgment, prepare written objections and a proposed order to facilitate a ruling on your objections.
- Limit your objections to those that are truly important to the case.
- Be aware of the irritating effect that constant objections have on the jury and the court.
- Object to allow the trial court and opposing counsel to correct their mistakes.
- If you have a new objection on different grounds, make a fresh objection to cover it.
- Make a timely motion to strike if objectionable evidence has been admitted.
- Don't overload the court with voluminous motions *in limine.*
- Don't file a motion *in limine* simply to keep out unfavorable evidence.
- Be careful with continuing objections; err on the side of renewing an objection at the appropriate time if you have any doubts.
- Get all objections and rulings on the record!

CHAPTER 5. COMMON LAW AND MOTION PROBLEMS

An all too familiar scenario: *You have just been served with a demurrer. You consider this the first salvo in the battle and you are prepared to oppose it whether it is well taken or not. When you lose the demurrer and are not given an opportunity to amend your complaint, you want to appeal immediately.*

The same morning, you also receive a motion for summary judgment on an important case. The motion is supported by an expert declaration that you don't find persuasive. You decide the best approach is simply to oppose the motion, relying on your client's deposition testimony. After you are served with the order granting the motion for summary judgment, you want to rush out and file an appeal from that ruling.

Are you being too impatient in one or both cases?

I. Demurrers:

72 Appeal from a judgment after a demurrer is sustained without leave to amend.

An appeal is generally taken from a final judgment, but that doesn't necessarily mean the parties have had their day in court. Sometimes a case is cut short by motions that effectively terminate the case, and a judgment of dismissal is then entered after the order granting the terminating motion. These motions could be a motion to quash, demurrer, motion to strike, motion for judgment on the pleadings, a motion for summary judgment, and dismissal motions. On the plus side, the appellant enjoys the benefit of California public policy that seeks to dispose of cases on their merits. Reviewing courts tend to be more skeptical of appeals from judgments that precluded a trial.

73 Consider whether you *really* want to file that demurrer.

In law school, we were taught that demurrers were disfavored and you shouldn't file one unless it would eliminate a cause of action or complaint. If it didn't, then you were just educating your opponent about how to remedy his or her pleadings, sometimes at a crucial phase of the proceedings. That advice still holds true today. Attorneys often view a demurrer as either a "billable event" or just a battle in an ongoing war. If you win this pleading battle, does that necessarily mean you will succeed at trial? Would you feel triumphant if your demurrer is sustained, only to face a new amended (and improved) pleading?

74 Recognize the different types of demurrers.

Through the years, I have observed three different types of demurrers:

1. A demurrer that attacks pleading defects that can be remedied;
2. A demurrer that attacks pleading defects and presents a true question of law;
3. A demurrer that attacks the pleading based on a question of law that no amendment can remedy.

If you are preparing the complaint and have done your homework as to what must be alleged to constitute a cause of action, then theoretically you will never face a demurrer that attacks pleading defects. While I don't necessarily stick to a form book for my entire pleading, I will use it as a checklist to make sure all necessary allegations are present.

75 Bullet-proof your complaint before going up on appeal.

Okay, so you have filed your pleading and the other side responds by filing a demurrer that claims you have omitted crucial allegations. Now the battle begins. But if you haven't alleged that crucial allegation, why fight it? Use the demurrer as a learning experience, even a checklist, and fix up your complaint. You might just call the other side and tell them that an amended complaint will be filed, making the demurrer moot. Or just file it before the hearing. (That doesn't mean allowing the court to work up the demurrer papers and then filing the amended pleading at the last minute.) In my opinion, there is no good reason to fight a demurrer on procedural defects; it only costs the clients money and gives you more work to do. Your time is better spent on amending the pleading. If you are facing a demurrer that has both pleading defects and an appealable question of law, then I would still clean up the pleading so that it looks as great as possible. Now you are ready to fight the real issue. You don't want to go to the appellate court with a sloppy pleading, even if the issue can't be cured by amendment. If your pleading is as good as it gets, then fight it on the legal issue. It could be an issue of standing to bring the action or the application of the statute of limitations, but the issue can't be resolved at the lower trial level. And no matter how well written your pleading is, you won't be able to avoid a review of your pleading at the appellate level to see if it states a cause of action.

76 Consider whether to amend your complaint before standing your ground.

At the hearing on the demurrer, you will likely find the trial court is liberal in granting leave to amend, especially if the defects can be remedied by more comprehensive allegations. Some judges want to avoid several rounds of pleadings and demurrers by inquiring if and how you can amend the pleadings. Always take that opportunity to explain how the pleading can be amended. And if the court seems indifferent to the possibility of amendment, ask for it. If given the chance, take the lead in describing to the trial court how the complaint can be amended. If the trial court determines that no amendment will overcome the defects in your pleading, then you are going up to the appellate court.

77 Appeal from the judgment of dismissal, not the order sustaining the demurrer without leave to amend.

If the order sustaining the demurrer without leave to amend eliminates all causes of action and disposes of the matter between the parties, then you will have to appeal to get back into court. But don't rush it and try to appeal from the order sustaining the demurrer. It is not an appealable order. You must appeal from the judgment of dismissal that follows the order. (*Leader v. Health Industries of America, Inc.* (2001) 89 Cal.App.4th 603, 611; *Farwell v. Sunset Mesa Property Owners Assn., Inc.* (2008) 163 Cal.App.4th 1545, 1551, fn. 4.) The judgment of dismissal may be submitted with the order, but it may also take days or weeks for it to be submitted to the trial court. If, however, the order does not dispose of all causes of action, you will have to decide whether to file a writ petition, continue to trial on the remaining causes of action, or dismiss the causes of action that remain alive. Keep in mind that your chances with a writ petition are minimal. "Appeal is presumed to be an adequate remedy, and writ review is rarely granted unless a significant issue of law is raised or resolution of the issue would result in a final disposition as to the petitioner." (*Cryolife, Inc. v. Superior Court* (2003) 110 Cal. App.4th 1145, 1151.)

78 The court of appeal conducts an independent review of a judgment of dismissal after an order sustaining the demurrer without leave to amend.

The appellate court conducts an independent or de novo review of the judgment of dismissal, including the substantive issues. (*TracFone Wireless, Inc. v. County of Los Angeles* (2008) 163 Cal.App.4th 1359, 1363.) The court will determine if you can state facts sufficient to constitute a cause of action under any legal theory. (*Unruh-Haxton v. Regents of University of California* (2008) 162 Cal. App.4th 343, 349.) This standard of review is one that is favored by appellate attorneys and is quite helpful to plaintiffs who might have pled a legal theory that isn't supported by the facts, but later discover a better legal theory that applies. That also means the appellate court is not that concerned with the ruling below; you can ask for review as if you never appeared before the trial court. That does not mean that the appellate court has no interest in what the trial court ruled, but its order is not binding on the appellate court and it will not stop them from looking at it anew. (*Holiday Matinee, Inc. v. Rambus, Inc.* (2004) 118 Cal.App.4th 1413, 1421.) The appellate court generally ignores the trial court's reasoning (as opposed to its ruling), and fortunately for the appellant, it is not limited by the theories raised in the pleading. (*Community Assisting Recovery, Inc. v. Aegis Security Ins. Co.* (2001) 92 Cal.App.4th 886, 891.)

79 The appellate court reviews the denial of leave to amend on an abuse of discretion standard.

If the plaintiff is also arguing that the trial court erred in granting leave to amend, that challenge is reviewed on an abuse of discretion standard. Whether the trial court has abused its discretion in denying leave to amend the complaint is tied to the appellate court's determination of whether the plaintiff can state a cause of action under any legal theory. If the plaintiff can, then denying leave to amend is an abuse of discretion. "And when it is sustained without leave to amend, we decide whether there is a reasonable possibility that the defect can be cured by amendment; if it can be, the trial court has abused its discretion and we reverse; if not, there has been no abuse of discretion and we affirm." (*Moreno v. Sanchez* (2003) 106 Cal.App.4th 1415, 1423.)

80 Don't fall into the trap of arguing evidence in a hearing on a demurrer.

A demurrer lies from defects on the face of the pleading or from facts that the court may judicially notice. (*Stevens v. Superior Court* (1999) 75 Cal.App.4th 594, 601.) A demurrer is not the place to challenge disputed facts. "[A] hearing on demurrer cannot be turned into a contested evidentiary hearing." (*Unruh-Haxton v. Regents of University of California* (2008) 162 Cal.App.4th 343, 365.) You know the defendant is attempting to do this when he or she explains your allegations or rebuts them with facts that they would present at trial. Another indication that defendant is resorting to extrinsic facts is when the demurrer is supported by a declaration. If the demurrer is truly testing the pleading or judicially noticed facts, then the filing of a declaration is unnecessary unless it is required to explain the request for judicial notice.

81 Don't argue at the demurrer hearing that you can prove your allegations at trial.

In reviewing your complaint, the appellate court is not concerned with how, or even if, you can prove your allegations at trial. "We do not concern ourselves with whether the plaintiff will be able to prove the facts which it alleges in the complaint." (*Canton Poultry & Deli, Inc. v. Stockwell, Harris, Widom & Woolverton* (2003) 109 Cal.App.4th 1219, 1226; *N.V. Heathorn, Inc. v County of San Mateo* (2005) 126 Cal.App.4th 1526, 1531.) The appellate court will also ignore erroneous or confusing labels or captions by the pleader; it is focusing on the facts alleged. (*Sunset Drive Corp. v. City of Redlands* (1999) 73 Cal.App.4th 215, 218-219; *Ananda Church of Self-Realization v. Massachusetts Bay Ins. Co.* (2002) 95 Cal.App.4th 1273, 1281.) Thus, the defendant cannot set forth arguments in their demurrer that, if proven true, would defeat plaintiff's complaint. (*Gould v. Maryland Sound Industries, Inc.* (1995) 31 Cal.App.4th 1137, 1144.) The court will presume that you can prove the facts you have alleged. (*Hill v. City of Santa Barbara* (1961) 196 Cal.App.2d 580, 585.)

82 Understand how the appellate court construes your complaint.

On review, the appellate court liberally construes the pleading in a reasonable manner. The appellate court is trying to determine if you can state a cause of action. It will liberally construe the pleading so as to achieve substantial justice, rather than summarily dispose of a defective pleading that can be salvaged. Thus, it will read the complaint in a reasonable manner, putting the allegations in context, and consider judicially noticed matter. (*Leonte v. ACS State and Local Solutions, Inc.* (2004) 123 Cal.App.4th 521, 525; *Page v. Los Angeles County Probation Dept.* (2004) 123 Cal.App.4th 1135, 1141.)

83 Use the appellate court's assumption of the truth of your allegations to your favor.

For purposes of appeal, the appellate court assumes the truth of your allegations. If you allege facts in your pleading, and they are not contradicted by your exhibits and judicially noticed documents, then the court will assume the truth of your allegations. (*California Public Employees' Retirement System v. Superior Court* (2008) 160 Cal. App.4th 174, 178, disapproved of on other grounds in *State Bd. of Chiropractic Examiners v. Superior Court* (2009) 45 Cal.4th 963; *Leonte v. ACS State and Local Solutions, Inc.* (2004) 123 Cal.App.4th 521, 525.) That assumption goes beyond the specific allegations. The appellate court will also assume the truth of facts that may be implied or reasonably inferred from the express allegations. (*Buller v. Sutter Health* (2008) 160 Cal.App.4th 981, 985-986.) However, if the allegations are contrary to law, the exhibits, or judicially noticed documents, they will be ignored. (*Consumer Cause, Inc. v. Weider Nutrition Internat., Inc.* (2001) 92 Cal.App.4th 363, 367.) And finally, if you have facts but you forget to put them into the complaint, they are not presumed to exist. (*Kramer v. Intuit Inc.* (2004) 121 Cal.App.4th 574, 578.)

84 The appellate court will not assume the truth of contentions, deductions, or conclusions of law or fact.

The appellate court will not assume the truth of contentions, deductions, or conclusions of law or fact. (*Levi v. O'Connell* (2006) 144 Cal.App.4th 700, 705.) Of course, that could prove to be a benefit to you or an obstacle. If you have included contentions and deductions in your pleading, then the court will ignore them, but if the defendant, in preparing the demurrer, is depending on contentions or deductions, then they will also be ignored.

85 You can argue for the first time on appeal that the complaint can be amended.

A real plus for appellants is that this argument can be raised for the first time on appeal. This is especially helpful since the appellate attorney may uncover new allegations and theories that would have been more appropriate and will overcome a defective complaint. Don't worry, life is not over! For while the appellant bears the burden of proving that the complaint can be amended to state facts constituting a cause of action and generally you cannot raise new issues on appeal, that argument can be made for the first time on appeal. (*Banis Restaurant Design, Inc. v. Serrano* (2005) 134 Cal.App.4th 1035, 1039.) (This rule is an exception to standard appellate procedure.) You can advance a new legal theory on appeal because the argument involves a pure question of fact that is presented by the undisputed facts. (*Dudley v. Department of Transportation* (2001) 90 Cal.App.4th 255, 259.) There is also authority to suggest that the appellate court can raise this issue even if you overlook it, but don't count on the appellate court to always do your work for you. (*City of Stockton v. Superior Court* (2007) 42 Cal.4th 730, 746.)

II. Motions for Summary Judgment

86 Be prepared to oppose motions for summary judgment.

Finding a motion for summary judgment in your mailbox usually produces a certain amount of stress. It may mean that you will be interrupting your well-planned (and tight) schedule by putting aside a large block of time devoted to opposing the motion. Or it could mean that now you have to scramble to find an expert who will review your case and submit a declaration opposing the motion. Or it reminds you of the discovery you put aside and now must tackle. I am always surprised that attorneys are surprised (and unprepared) when they are served with motions for summary judgment. From the date you are first retained, you should anticipate a motion for summary judgment as part of the litigation process and plan on how you will oppose it. While once carefully scrutinized and disfavored by trial courts, these motions increasingly are being granted as a means of ridding busy courtrooms of cases that don't require a trial to determine the winner. We see them in cases that were on track for trial, such as medical malpractice or wrongful termination cases. A plaintiff's attorney should not ignore the possibility of receiving a motion for summary judgment and should not be placed in the position of hunting down declarations, especially expert declarations that require a review of documents, while the clock is ticking. In addition, if your client or a witness gives damaging testimony during a deposition, get the correct testimony on record *at that time*. You do not want to file a declaration in the summary judgment motion that conflicts with a prior deposition. It will be disregarded. "Where a party's self-serving declarations contradict credible discovery admissions and purport to impeach that party's own prior sworn testimony, they should be disregarded." (*Archdale v. American International Specialty Lines Ins. Co.* (2007) 154 Cal.App.4th 449, 473; *D'Amico v. Board of Medical Examiners* (1974) 11 Cal.3d 1, 20-22.)

87 Make sure your motion for summary judgment tells a story with a beginning, middle, and end.

Some attorneys suffer from tunnel vision when it comes to their cases. They have lived with their cases for months, even years, and may be thoroughly familiar with the facts. But now you are dealing with someone – a judge with an enormous caseload – who doesn't know your case. Research has shown that humans are wired to think in terms of stories; this is how we make sense of and organize information. The motion, from the Introduction to the Statement of Facts to the Conclusion, must present a story that answers the questions and leads the reader to the inescapable conclusion that the opposing party can't point to the existence of one triable issue of material fact, can't prove one element of a cause of action, and can't defeat an affirmative defense. For example, don't focus on a breach without describing the contract, and don't focus on the injuries a plaintiff sustained without first setting the scene, including the cause of the accident. When your case is up on appeal, you want your motion to present the story – the entire story – and not leave anything out. The court of appeal has less familiarity with the case and the parties, and no judge or justice likes to feel that they are only seeing one piece of a big puzzle.

88 Make it easy for the trial court, and the court of appeal, to give you what you want.

Whether you are the moving or opposing party, you want to make the trial court's task in reviewing the motion for summary judgment as easy as possible. That means having a clear and concise Introduction, topic headings that are fairly descriptive of the argument, and a presentation that is easy on the eyes. To me, that includes shorter sentences with active verbs, and shorter paragraphs. Variety is the spice of life, and I think this rule applies to sentence structure. I also make sure that I throw in a few indented quotes to mix up the structure so the judge isn't facing the monotony of page after page with no change in format. Judges are often overworked and saddled with large caseloads. Your case is not the only case on the calendar. Don't expect them to know your case as well as you do or recall the last hearing. You are lucky if they do, but if they don't, they may not want to admit it. That means making your motion as comprehensive as possible. That also means presenting it in a way that doesn't require the court to hunt for documents or evidence. This suggestion could apply to something as simple as tabbing and indexing your evidence. Tabs make everyone's life easy. It also means not referring to evidence in your memorandum of points and authorities, and then avoiding it when preparing the Separate Statement. And finally, keep your page count to a respectable level by trying to stay focused and not bringing up matters that will only complicate the motion. Complications work against a moving party as the trial court may suspect there is a triable issue lurking somewhere; it just hasn't found out where it is.

89 **Don't overload the trial court with unnecessary objections.**

Although California Rules of Court, rule 3.1352 allows for either written or oral objections, without question, I would recommend preparing written objections rather than relying on making them at the hearing. "Part of the judicial function in assessing the merits of a summary judgment or adjudication motion involves a determination as to what evidence is admissible and that which is not." (*City of Long Beach v. Farmers & Merchants Bank of Long Beach* (2000) 81 Cal. App.4th 780, 784, overruled on other grounds in *Reid v. Google* (2010) 50 Cal.4th 512.) If the judge is going to review the paperwork well in advance of the hearing, wouldn't you prefer giving the judge your objections at that time, rather than waiting until the last minute?

Code of Civil Procedure section 437c(b)(5) provides "Evidentiary objections not made at the hearing shall be deemed waived." Code of Civil Procedure section 437c(d) requires that objections based on the failure to comply with the requirement that the affidavits or declarations shall be made on personal knowledge "shall be made at the hearing or shall be deemed waived." (See *Reid v. Google, supra,* for a comprehensive discussion as to what is meant by the statement that objections "shall be made at the hearing or shall be deemed waived," as provided for in Code of Civil Procedure section 437c.)

90 **Be familiar with the rules for objecting in motions for summary judgments.**

California Rules of Court, Rule 3.1352 provides:

> "Any party desiring to make objections to evidence in the papers on a motion for summary judgment must either:
>
> (1) Submit objections in writing under rule 3.1354; or
> (2) Make arrangements for a court reporter to be present at the hearing."

While the presence of the court reporter and reporting of the hearing ensures that a record is made of the objection, it still does not give the court advance warning to consider the objections when it is reviewing the motion papers.

91 File written objections in the motion for summary judgment.

If you decide to file written objections with your papers, they must be served or filed at the same time that your opposition or reply are served and filed "[u]nless otherwise excused by the court on a showing of good cause, . . ." (Cal. Rules of Court, rule 3.1354(a).) The format for written objections is also found in California Rules of Court, rule 3.1354. You should stick to that format without deviation. Just the other day, I was consulted by an attorney who showed me a tentative ruling by a judge who refused to consider written objections because they were not in proper format. One moving party won his motion for summary judgment because the judge sustained objections to the expert's declaration, while the other moving party lost the motion because the objections were not in proper format, and as a consequence, were not considered by the judge. You don't always know whether you have a judge who is a stickler for the rules or one who looks beyond minor procedural errors. Don't take that chance and you will be safe from procedural attacks.

92 Learn the proper format for written objections.

The format for written objections is set forth in California Rules of Court, rule 3.1354(b) as follows:

> **"(b) Format of objections**
>
> All written objections to evidence must be served and filed separately from the other papers in support of or in opposition to the motion. Objections on specific evidence may be referenced by the objection number in the right column of a separate statement in opposition or reply to a motion, but the

objections must not be restated or reargued in the separate statement. Each written objection must be numbered consecutively and must:

(1) Identify the name of the document in which the specific material objected to is located;

(2) State the exhibit, title, page, and line number of the material objected to;

(3) Quote or set forth the objectionable statement or material; and

(4) State the grounds for each objection to that statement or material.

Written objections to evidence must follow one of the following two formats:

(First Format):

Objections to Jackson Declaration

Objection Number 1

"Johnson told me that no widgets were ever received." (Jackson declaration, page 3, lines 7-8.)
Grounds for Objection 1: Hearsay (Evid. Code, § 1200); lack of personal knowledge (Evid. Code, § 702(a).

Objection Number 2

"A lot of people find widgets to be very useful." (Jackson declaration, page 17, line 5.)
Grounds for Objection 2: Irrelevant (Evid. Code, §§ 210, 350-351).

(Second Format):

Objections to Jackson Declaration

Material Objected to:	**Grounds for Objection:**
1. Jackson declaration, page 3, lines 7-8: "Johnson told me that no widgets were ever received."	Hearsay (Evid. Code, § 1200); lack of personal knowledge (Evid. Code, § 702(a).)
2. Jackson declaration, page 17, line 5: "A lot of people find widgets to be very useful."	Irrelevant (Evid. Code, §§ 210, 350-351.)

(c) Proposed order

A party submitting written objections to evidence must submit with the objections a proposed order. The proposed order must include places for the court to indicate whether it has sustained or overruled each objection. It must also include a place for the signature of the judge. The proposed order must be in one of the following two formats:

(First Format):

Objections to Jackson Declaration

Objection Number 1

"Johnson told me that no widgets were ever received." (Jackson declaration, page 3, lines 7-8.)
Grounds for Objection 1: Hearsay (Evid. Code, § 1200; lack of personal knowledge (Evid. Code, § 702(a).)

Court's Ruling on Objection 1: Sustained: ________
Overruled: ________

Objection Number 2

"A lot of people find widgets to be very useful." (Jackson declaration, page 17, line 5.)
Grounds for Objection 2: Irrelevant (Evid. Code, §§ 210, 350-351.)

Court's Ruling on Objection 2: Sustained: ________
Overruled: ________

(Second Format):

Objections to Jackson Declaration

Material Objected to:	Grounds for Objection:	Ruling on the Objection:
1. Jackson declaration, page 3, lines 7-8: "Johnson told me that no widgets were ever received."	Hearsay (Evid. Code, § 1200); lack of personal knowledge (Evid. Code, § 702(a).)	Sustained: _____ Overruled: _____
2. Jackson declaration, page 17, line 5: "A lot of people find widgets to be very useful."	Irrelevant (Evid. Code, §§ 210, 350-351.)	Sustained: _____ Overruled: _____

Date: _______________ ___________________________
Judge

93 Object only when it is important to the case.

Even though you have the right to make objections, I would recommend that you be judicious in the amount of objections you make. Determine whether it is really important to the issues in the case. Before the new rules required attorneys to submit a proposed order that allowed the judge to check off "overruled" or "sustained," a voluminous amount of objections always made it difficult for the judge to rule. Now that task is much easier but if you really want to make life easy for the judge, stick to objections that have merit and will ultimately affect the motion. In 2009, the First Appellate District took an opportunity to warn attorneys and judges about the abuses that plague motions for summary judgment in *Nazir v. United Airlines, Inc.* (2009) 178 Cal.App.4th 243. Here are a few examples:

- The motion sought summary adjudication of 44 issues, but more than half failed to meet the moving party's burden under Code Civ. Proc., §437c(f)(1) because they did not completely dispose of a cause of action.
- The moving party's separate statement consisted of 196 facts, with numerous repetition of the same facts, many of which were not material to the issues.
- The reply papers included a 297-page separate statement, which is not provided for by statute.
- Defendant's reply included 764 objections to plaintiff's evidence, contained in 324 pages. The court was extremely critical of this approach, noting that it imposed a huge burden on the trial court and was hardly "good advocacy." (*Id.* at p. 254, fn. 3.)
- Of defendant's 764 objections, some did

not even assert a basis for objection or, as with 250 objections, the defendant failed to quote the evidence objected to in violation of California Rules of Court, rule 3.1354. (*Id.* at p. 256.)

- Some of defendant's objections were to plaintiff's brief, not his evidence, and were frivolous.
- The court warned against the practice of having multiple attorneys assigned to work on a motion, with the most junior lawyer handling the objections. "Perhaps a wiser practice would be to have the most experienced lawyer, presumably with a better understanding of the law of evidence, deal with the objections." (*Id.* at p. 257, fn. 6.)
- The parties submitted over 2,200 pages of separate statements and 764 objections in 325 pages. "The incredible volume of material here simply has no place in a system where overburdened trial courts labor long and hard. Thus, we conclude with some guidance in the event a trial court is ever again confronted with anything remotely close to that here." (*Id.* at p. 289.)
- The court was critical of plaintiff's presentation, concluding it was misleading and an attempt to hide the real issues.

This case should serve as a warning to counsel in preparing either your moving or opposition papers. Limit the facts in your separate statement to material facts, and limit your objections to relevant objections, setting forth the proper grounds and complying with California Rules of Court, rule 3.1352 and rule 3.1354. Finally, make every attempt to make it easy on the trial court to give you what you want.

94 Whenever possible, obtain rulings on your objections or requests for judicial notice.

One of the biggest problems I encounter in dealing with summary judgments is the trial attorney's failure to obtain rulings on his or her objections. Of course, California Rules of Court, rule 3.1354(b) and (c) make it easy for the judge to simply check off a ruling, but I would still recommend keeping your objections to a minimum and making sure they really make a difference to your case. In ruling on the motion for summary judgment, the court must "consider all of the evidence," except that evidence to which objections have been made and sustained, as well as inferences reasonably drawn from that evidence. (Code Civil Proc., § 437c(c).) The court must view all evidence and inferences "in the light most favorable to the opposing party." (*Aguilar v. Atlantic Richfield Co.* (2001) 25 Cal.4th 826, 843.) The court has a duty to rule on evidentiary objections, but no one wants to be the attorney arguing that the judge is shirking his or her judicial duties by failing to rule. "Trial courts have a duty to rule on evidentiary objections. Part of the judicial function in assessing the merits of a summary judgment or adjudication motion involves a determination as to what evidence is admissible and that which is not." (*City of Long Beach v. Farmers & Merchants Bank of Long Beach* (2000) 81 Cal.App.4th 780, 784, overruled on other grounds in *Reid v. Google* (2010) 50 Cal.4th 512.) "A trial court cannot decide whether a motion should be denied or granted until it has first determined what admissible evidence is in play on the motion." (*Vineyard Springs Estates, LLC v. Superior Court* (2004) 120 Cal.App.4th 633, 642.) To help focus the argument at the hearing, you might ask the trial court to first rule on the objections.

95 Be familiar with the recent Supreme Court ruling in *Reid v. Google.*

In the old days when I started practicing, it was not uncommon for a trial judge to avoid ruling on specific objections, and tell you instead that he or she would only consider admissible evidence and disregard inadmissible evidence. Sounds smart, I suppose, but it really doesn't give the court of appeal a sufficient record to review. This rule was announced in *Biljac Associates v. First Interstate Bank* (1990) 218 Cal.App.3d 1410, which rejected the requirement of express rulings, especially since the court of appeal reviews the matter de novo. The court in *Biljac* stated, "[B]eing able to identify particular flaws in the lower court's reasoning has no value because, as appellants themselves note, summary judgment must be upheld if correct on any ground regardless of wrong 'reasons' which may have guided the court . . . More generally, it is presumed on appeal that a judgment has not relied on irrelevant or incompetent evidence." (*Id.* at pp. 1419-1420; citation omitted.) (See Strategic Tool, No. 56.)

This rule in *Biljac* had been overruled, superseded and disagreed with so many times that you might has well ignore the holding; however, it was re-examined in the California Supreme Court's recent decision in *Reid v. Google* (2010) 50 Cal.4th 512. We've been waiting for the Court to address this issue for several years and now they have. In that decision, the Court recognized that "the *Biljac* procedure itself was designed to ease the extreme burden on trial courts when all 'too often' 'litigants file blunderbuss objections to virtually every item of evidence submitted.'" (*Reid v. Google, supra,* at p. 532, citing from *Demps v. San Francisco Housing Authority* (2007) 149 Cal.App.4th 564, 578, fn. 6.)

In *Reid,* an age discrimination and wrongful termination case, Google filed 31 pages of written objections to Reid's evidence in opposition to Google's motion for summary judgment. The trial court failed to rule on the objections, stating it was relying only "on competent and admissible evidence." (*Id.* at p. 520.) The Court of

Appeal concluded the trial court's failure to rule on the evidentiary objections did not waive those objections on appeal, finding that the filing of written evidentiary objections before the summary judgment hearing was sufficient to preserve the objections. (This rule seems to be restricted to motions for summary judgment or adjudication.)

The California Supreme Court held:

> "We agree with the Court of Appeal's conclusions. Regarding the waiver issue, the Court of Appeal correctly determined that a finding of waiver does not depend on whether a trial court rules expressly on evidentiary objections and that Google's filing of written evidentiary objections before the summary judgment hearing preserved them on appeal. (Code Civ. Proc., § 437c, subds. (b)(5), (d).) After a party objects to evidence, the trial court must then rule on those objections. If the trial court fails to rule after a party has properly objected, the evidentiary objections are not deemed waived on appeal."

(*Id.* at p. 517.)

The Court further found that trial courts are required to consider all admissible evidence and the rules of waiver do not apply in summary judgment proceedings. California Rules of Court, rule 3.1352 covers how objections can be made: either in writing pursuant to rule 3.1354, or by making arrangements to have a court reporter present at the hearing. Rule 3.1354 also requires that a party submitting written objections must also submit a proposed order, which would allow the trial court to indicate whether it was sustaining and overruling each objection. Thus, objections are deemed made "at the hearing" for purposes of Code of Civil Procedure section 437c, subdivisions (b)(5) and (d), thus avoiding a waiver. In addition, the Court disapproved of *Biljac* "to the extent it permits the trial court to avoid ruling on specific evidentiary objections" (*Id.* at p. 532, fn. 8.), and confirmed that if the trial court failed to rule on objections, it is presumed the objections have been overruled, the trial court considered the evidence in making its rulings, and the objections are preserved on appeal. (*Id.* at p. 534.) As a result, even if the trial court fails to rule on those objections, they are preserved for review on appeal.

96 Prepare your declarations according to the Code of Civil Procedure section 2015.5.

A motion for summary judgment or opposition thereto may be supported by "affidavits, declarations admissions, answers to interrogatories, depositions, and matter of which judicial notice shall or may be taken." (Code Civ. Proc., § 437c(b)(1).) Subsection 437c(d) also requires that "[s]upporting and opposing affidavits or declarations shall be made by any person on personal knowledge, shall set forth admissible evidence, and shall show affirmatively that the affiant is competent to testify to the matters stated in the affidavits or declarations. Any objections based on the failure to comply with the requirements of this subdivision shall be made at the hearing or shall be deemed waived." The form of declarations is governed by Code of Civil Procedure section 2015.5, which requires that the declaration "recites that it is certified or declared by him or her to be true under penalty of perjury, is subscribed by him or her, and (1), if executed within this state, states the date and place of execution, or (2), if executed at any place, within or without this state, states the date of execution and that it is so certified or declared under the laws of the State of California. The certification or declaration may be in substantially the following form:

(a) If executed within this state:
"I certify (or declare) under penalty of perjury that the foregoing is true and correct:"

________________ __________________________

(Date and Place) (Signature)

(b) If executed at any place, within or without this state:
"I certify (or declare) under penalty of perjury under the laws of the State of California that the foregoing is true and correct":

________________ __________________________

(Date) (Signature)

If the declaration is executed outside of California but fails to include the language "under the laws of the State of California" as indicated in option (b) above, then the declaration will be considered to be inadmissible hearsay. "[C]ourts do not find compliance with section 2015.5 to be both substantial and sufficient unless all statutory conditions appear on the face of the declaration in some form." (*Kulshrestha v. First Union Commercial Corp.* (2004) 33 Cal.4th 601, 612.) Add these certifications to every declaration that is prepared, and if it doesn't exist in your opponent's declarations, be sure to object. As a final note, make sure the declarations do not conflict with previous sworn deposition or discovery responses. (*Archdale v. American International Specialty Lines Ins. Co.* (2007) 154 Cal. App.4th 449, 473; *D'Amico v. Board of Medical Examiners* (1974) 11 Cal.3d 1, 20-22.)

97 Adding the statement that the evidence is within the witness's personal knowledge won't hurt.

Many attorneys will add a variation of the following statement: "The foregoing is within my personal knowledge, and as such, I am competent to testify thereto." Don't rely on the belief that simply adding this statement is enough to avoid scrutiny or objections. Code of Civil Procedure section 437c(d) requires admissible evidence and declarations "shall show *affirmatively that the affiant is competent to testify.*" In preparing declarations, make sure the body of the declaration reflects that personal knowledge. If the declarant was present at a face-to-face conference or personally observed something, the declaration should be tailored to show that the declarant possesses that personal knowledge. Declarations often run rampant with hearsay, and attorneys believe it might be worth the risk of including hearsay statements, hoping that the opposition might not object. I believe it is better to avoid including hearsay statements, which might weaken the credibility of the declaration. Whenever possible, you should draft the declaration with a view to avoiding a hearsay objection, or state facts that will support an exception to the hearsay rule.

98 **A bare claim of personal knowledge in declarations may be ignored by the courts.**

Conversely, when you are reviewing an opposing party's declarations, don't simply accept the declarant's statement as absolute proof that the declarant has personal knowledge. "Where the facts stated do not themselves show it, such bare statement of the affiant has no redeeming value and should be ignored." (*Snider v. Snider* (1962) 200 Cal.App.2d 741, 754; *Mamou v. Trendwest Resorts, Inc.* (2008) 165 Cal. App.4th 686, 692, fn. 1.) Even so, while others have indicated that the omission of this form statement is immaterial, I prefer to keep it in for several reasons. One, I think courts are so accustomed to seeing it that if the statement is missing, they may suspect the declarant lacks personal knowledge, and two, it is a confirmation of personal knowledge when the language in the declaration may not clearly indicate such knowledge.

99 Scrutinize the language in the declaration to determine if it is possible for the declarant to have personal knowledge of the facts alleged.

Think about what the declarant is stating. Sometimes attorneys will take the easy way out, and rather than getting more declarations, they will seek to have as few declarations as possible. For instance, if someone is testifying to a situation that occurred at the workplace, but then states he or she began working at the company after the event, it would appear the declarant can't possibly possess personal knowledge of the facts stated in the declaration. A similar situation might arise where the declarant works out of the main out-of-state office of a company and yet purports to describe a situation occurring at a local branch office.

100 Analyze the language used in the declaration.

Be careful of the language used. For instance, the words "I learned," "I discovered," "I believe," or "I am informed," may indicate a lack of personal knowledge and should be objected to. "The phrase 'To the best of my knowledge' indicates something less than the 'personal knowledge' required under Code of Civil Procedure section 437c, and implies that the declarant's statement is based on something similar to information and belief." (*Bowden v. Robinson* (1977) 67 Cal. App.3d 705, 719-720.) "Declarations based on information and belief are insufficient to satisfy the burden of either the moving or opposing party on a motion for summary judgment or adjudication." (*Lopez v. University Partners* (1997) 54 Cal. App.4th 1117, 1124.)

101 You must controvert statements made in declarations or they will be accepted as true.

Keep in mind that declarations that are not controverted must be accepted as true for purposes of the motion. (Code Civil Proc., § 437c(e).) The trial judge cannot deny the motion because he or she suspects the statements lack credibility. The judge may deny the motion for summary judgment if the opposing party is unable to controvert the declarations; however, this is a discretionary call on the judge's part. Subsection 437c(e) provides, "If a party is otherwise entitled to a summary judgment pursuant to this section, summary judgment may not be denied on grounds of credibility or for want of cross-examination of witnesses furnishing affidavits or declarations in support of the summary judgment, except that summary judgment may be denied in the discretion of the court, where the only proof of a material fact offered in support of the summary judgment is an affidavit or declaration made by an individual who was the sole witness to the fact; or where a material fact is an individual's state of mind, or lack thereof, and that fact is sought to be established solely by the individual's affirmation thereof." These circumstances may arise where the declarant is the sole witness to a fact or the declaration is addressing the declarant's statement of mind, particularly as to intent. (*Meighan v. Shore* (1995) 34 Cal.App.4th 1025, 1046; *KOVR-TV, Inc. v. Superior Court* (1995) 31 Cal.App.4th 1023, 1031.)

102 Look for defects in expert witness declarations.

If an expert testimony would be required on an issue at trial, then an expert witness declaration is required to support or oppose a motion for summary judgment. (*Kelley v. Trunk* (1998) 66 Cal. App.4th 519, 523-524.) Establishing admissibility of an expert declaration is governed by similar rules that apply to expert testimony at trial. (Evid. Code §§ 720, *et seq.*) An expert's opinion that is based on speculation, conjecture or conclusions will be rejected as inadmissible. (Evid. Code § 801(b); *Mitchell v. United Nat. Ins. Co.* (2005) 127 Cal. App.4th 457, 478.) An expert declaration should contain the following:

- The expert's qualifications or competency to testify.
- What information the expert relied on in forming an opinion, including what documents or records were reviewed.
- A statement that the expert's opinion is based on matters that are reasonably relied upon by experts in forming their opinions.
- The factual basis for the opinion. "[A] n opinion unsupported by reasons or explanations does not establish the absence of a material fact issue for trial, as required for summary judgment." (*Kelley v. Trunk, supra,* at p. 524.) As noted in that case, the court or trier of fact may reject an expert's opinion if the reasons given for it are unsound. The court concluded, "It is not our intent to disparage either the summary judgment procedure, or its appropriate use in malpractice cases. The procedure is a long-established and important part of our civil system. Summary judgment is appropriate in every case where the statutory standard is met, and the absence of material issues for trial established. However, that standard is not satisfied by laconic expert declarations which provide only an ultimate opinion, unsupported by reasoned explanation." (*Id.*

at pp. 524-525.) However, in the case of *Hanson v. Grode* (1999) 76 Cal. App.4th 601, the Second Appellate District rejected *Kelley's* approach, declining to require the declarant to set forth details in "excruciating detail." (*Id.* at p. 608, fn. 6.)

- Supporting hospital records and testimony authenticating such records. In *Garibay v. Hemmat* (2008) 161 Cal.App.4th 735, the court concluded that an "expert's opinion based on assumptions of fact without evidentiary support has no evidentiary value." (*Id.* at p. 743.) As a result, the court rejected an expert declaration that did not include authenticated copies of the medical records.

Attorneys may wonder how much detail should be supplied. Too little and they run afoul of *Kelley v. Trunk, supra,* for failing to provide reasons for their conclusions. The expert declarant needs to avoid making conclusions, especially ones that may look like speculation or conjecture, which may occur if reasons aren't supplied. On the other hand, what is the disadvantage of overloading the court with too much detail or reasons? It is better to err on the side of providing too much information, although more information gives your opponent more potential ammunition. Unless you know the court's threshold on what it considers too much detail, it is better to make the expert declaration as complete as possible.

103 Don't overlook the importance of a proper separate statement.

The importance of the separate statement cannot be overlooked. Some judges will immediately review the separate statements, hoping to find what facts are undisputed and those that are not. Others will review it as the last document of the moving papers. One of the biggest hazards with preparing a separate statement is failing to make sure it (1) includes all of the facts necessary to support the evidence and (2) refers to the supporting evidence. See California Rules of Court, rule 3.1350(h) for the proper format. In reviewing a motion for summary judgment, I sometimes find that facts included in the declarations or memorandum of points and authorities fail to make their way into the separate statement. "When a fact upon which plaintiff relies is not mentioned in the separate statement, it is irrelevant that such fact might be buried in the mound of paperwork filed with the trial court; the court does not have the burden to conduct a search for facts that counsel failed to bring out." (*Lewis v. County of Sacramento* (2001) 93 Cal.App.4th 107, 116.)

104 Know the role of the separate statement in opposing a motion for summary judgment.

In opposing the motion, an opposing party often fails to realize that the separate statement serves different functions as to opposing parties. An opposition separate statement must respond to the material facts put forth in the moving papers by stating whether the fact is undisputed or disputed. If a fact is disputed, there should be a reference to the supporting evidence. "In opposing a defendant's motion for summary judgment, the plaintiff must submit a separate statement setting forth the specific facts showing that a trial issue of material fact exists . . . Without a separate statement of undisputed facts with references to supporting evidence in the form of affidavits or declarations, it is impossible for the plaintiff to demonstrate the existence of disputed facts." (Code Civ. Proc., § 437c(b)(3); Cal. Rules of Court, rules 3.1350(f) and (h); *Lewis v. County of Sacramento* (2001) 93 Cal.App.4th 107, 116.) As a secondary and very important function, the opposition separate statement must identify any material fact not mentioned in the moving papers that is disputed and creates a triable issue. Quite often an opposing attorney will simply respond to the separate statement prepared by the moving party. But a separate statement is an opportunity to show triable issues exist that justify denial of the motion. Of course, each fact must refer to the supporting evidence. When I am asked to review a motion for summary judgment by the opposing party, the first question I ask is what are the triable issues of fact. Then I look at the separate statement to confirm that they are listed. The existence of triable issues should also be repeated in your introduction to your memorandum of points and authorities. If it is not in either place, but scattered somewhere in your opposition papers, you have made the judge's task that much more difficult. Always try to make it easy for the judge to deny your opponent's motion for summary judgment.

105 Make a proper request for a continuance.

Problems frequently arise when an opposing party requires a continuance. If the opposing party demonstrates that essential evidence "may exist but cannot, for reasons stated, then be presented, the court shall deny the motion" or continue it. (Code Civ. Proc., § 437c(h).) The language in section 437c(h) is strong; the court is under a mandatory duty to deny or continue the motion if such facts *may* exist. But the code section requires an explanation or reasons why those facts cannot be then presented. It is preferable to have your discovery already scheduled at the same time the continuance is sought or advise the trial court how long it will take to produce the relevant evidence.

106 Don't wait until the date of the summary judgment hearing to ask for a continuance.

Quite often, an attorney seeking a continuance will submit a simple request for a continuance in his or her opposition, but do nothing about the request until the date of the hearing. However, Code of Civil Procedure section 437c(h) suggests that a request for a continuance may be made in the opposition papers or by ex parte motion *before* the opposition is due. (Code Civ. Proc., § 437c(h).) My preference is to ask for a continuance first by an ex parte application as soon as the need arises. I also recommend that it be done after you have taken some active steps to conduct the additional discovery, such as setting up depositions, etc. Taking the time to prepare an ex parte application may demonstrate that you really need to obtain additional discovery and the request is not just made because you are in danger of losing the motion. It also stops the court from reviewing the motion until it is ripe. Besides, no judge will want to read all of the papers only to find a request for continuance buried on the last page of a party's opposition.

107 Submit a comprehensive declaration with your request for a continuance.

The declaration in support of a request for a continuance must set forth what discovery is necessary to properly oppose the motion for summary judgment. This proposed discovery should be tied into your assertion that certain facts may exist that will result in a denial of the motion. The declaration should state why the information in the requested discovery is essential to oppose the motion and why additional time is needed. (*Combs v. Skyriver Communications, Inc.* (2008) 159 Cal.App.4th 1242, 1270.) When advising the court as to the specific reasons why the evidence cannot be presented either in the opposition or at the time of the hearing, be sure to include an estimate of the time necessary to obtain such evidence. That is one reason why I prefer to have the discovery already scheduled so that a date certain can be presented to the court. Statements, such as "further discovery is necessary," are simply not enough to support a continuance. "It is not sufficient under the statute merely to indicate further discovery or investigation is contemplated. The statute makes it a condition that the party moving for a continuance show 'facts essential to justify opposition may exist.'" (*Roth v. Rhodes* (1994) 25 Cal.App.4th 530, 548.) As stated in *Cooksey v. Alexakis* (2004) 123 Cal. App.4th 246, "A declaration in support of a request for continuance under section 437c, subdivision (h) must show: '(1) the facts to be obtained are essential to opposing the motion; (2) there is reason to believe such facts may exist; and (3) the reasons why additional time is needed to obtain these facts.'" (*Id.* at p. 254; citations omitted.)

108 Consider a motion for new trial after an order on the motion for summary judgment.

Odd as it may seem, you can bring a motion for new trial following a summary judgment. Most attorneys don't think of this post-trial motion as an option because there has been no trial, but the hearing is an adjudication of the case. "It may seem semantically anomalous to speak of a 'new trial' following summary judgment, which is a determination that there shall be no trial at all. In the light, however, of the rule that a motion for new trial lies after judgment on the pleadings, *Carney v. Simmons,* 49 Cal.2d 84 [315 P.2d 305], the procedure appears proper." (*Green v. Del-Camp Invest., Inc.* (1961) 193 Cal.App.2d 479, 481.) This rule also applies to motions for judgment on the pleadings and demurrers. (*Carney v. Simmons, supra,* at p. 91 and *Green v. Del-Camp Invest., Inc., supra.*) While it may seem an odd way to challenge a decision without a full trial on the merits, I have successfully made these motions in the past. (See Appendix E, Form 21 for a sample "Notice of Intention to Move for New Trial.")

~ Tips for Success ~

- Don't ignore the importance of California public policy of resolving cases on their merits.
- Avoid unnecessary pleading battles; don't demur just because you can.
- Be willing to use the demurrer as a checklist to strengthen your complaint.
- Be reasonable enough to amend your complaint if the demurrer is well taken and your complaint is defective.
- Before filing a demurrer, consider whether it will end the case or simply educate your opponent.
- Don't file a demurrer or motion for summary judgment just for the sake of increasing attorney's fees.
- Understand the principles applied by the trial court in construing the complaint.
- Clean up your complaint before you send it to the appellate court.
- If you later discover you can state a cause of action in your complaint, be sure to bring it up on appeal.
- When you take a case, be prepared for a motion for summary judgment and consider how to oppose it.
- Take an aggressive approach when opposing a motion for summary judgment.

- Object when necessary, but don't file voluminous and boilerplate objections.

- Make the motion for summary judgment or opposition tell a story that leads to the conclusion you want.

- Spend a lot of time analyzing the separate statement: check the facts and make sure the supporting evidence matches.

- If you are opposing a motion for summary judgment, put the "triable issue" in a prominent place in your documents, starting with the introduction, the memorandum of points and suthorities, and finally, in your separate statement.

- Don't wait to conduct discovery if you are served with a motion for summary judgment.

- Make a proper and fully supported request to continue a motion for summary judgment at your earliest opportunity.

- Enlist the aid of an appellate attorney to make sure you have raised all issues and protected the record.

- Consider making a motion for new trial if the demurrer is sustained without leave to amend or summary judgment is granted.

CHAPTER 6. THE COURT REPORTER

An all too familiar scenario: *You have engaged in a number of in-chambers or sidebar conferences during trial that resulted in some key rulings by the court. Because the judge seemed to be in a hurry to finish the trial, you failed to ask for a court reporter to be present for these conferences. As trial resumed, you didn't want to annoy the judge by repeating the stipulations and rulings made during the earlier conferences. You call your appellate attorney, who asks whether the conferences were somehow memorialized on the record. You explain the circumstances, including the pressures that you were under. The appellate attorney reads the transcripts and asks what the witness was referring to when she pointed at an exhibit.*

Now what happens?

I. In-chambers or sidebar conferences

109 Request that the court reporter be present for in-chambers or sidebar conferences.

During trial, unreported conferences often occur in the judge's chambers or during a sidebar conference. If you believe that a crucial issue will be discussed, you are entitled to ask that the court reporter be present to record the conference. (See Tool No. 113 below.) The judge or opposing counsel may be irritated by your request, but your primary goal is to protect the record. If you fail to record the conference, the reviewing court will presume the unreported proceedings would have shown the absence of error. If you are unable to have the reporter present in chambers or at sidebar, try to get the gist of the conference on record once you return to court or file a declaration with the court as to what happened.

110 Get any stipulations, objections or rulings made during an in-chambers or sidebar conference on the record.

One might imagine that an in-chambers or sidebar conference can be more relaxed or the attorneys may be more honest about what is happening at trial. The judge often takes off his or her robes and invites the attorneys to relax as well. The attorneys may see it as an opportunity to explain their positions away from the scrutiny of a jury or the public. But what happens during these conferences can be very important. Rulings can be made and stipulations entered into. If neither the conference nor the ruling/stipulation is entered on the record, it is almost the same as if it had never been made. While stipulations may seem an expeditious way of streamlining your trial, you may have waived your client's right to appeal. Get it on the record!

111 Summarize objections and rulings made in conferences outside the presence of the court reporter as soon as possible on the record.

Attorneys frequently ask what to do if such rulings are made outside the presence of the court reporter. You should be able to summarize the stipulation or ruling for the record without offending the judge. By repeating it, you may have a chance to clarify any problems and find out if there is a difference of opinion as to what was agreed upon. As noted in *Mary M. v. City of Los Angeles* (1991) 54 Cal.3d 202, 213, fn. 4, "Experienced litigators know that many trial courts conduct unreported instruction conferences and permit counsel to 'make their record' by recording their objections after the jury has retired to deliberate. This practice promotes judicial efficiency, because it allows matters to be placed on the record at a time when the jury will not be kept waiting."

112 Arrange for a court reporter for trial.

Trying to save money by not having a reporter present is being penny-wise, pound foolish. If your client does not want to arrange or pay for a court reporter for trial, it may be tantamount to waiving any right to appeal on certain grounds. It is as if the client is willing to rely solely on a single shot at justice. For example, if objections are not reported, it is as if they were never made. This failure is a death knell for substantial evidence appeals. "Where no reporter's transcript has been provided and no error is apparent on the face of the existing appellate record, the judgment must be *conclusively presumed correct* as to *all evidentiary matters.* To put it another way, it is presumed that the unreported trial testimony would demonstrate the absence of error. . . . The effect of this rule is that an appellant who attacks a judgment but supplies no reporter's transcript will be precluded from raising an argument as to the sufficiency of the evidence." (*Estate of Fain* (1999) 75 Cal.App.4th 973, 992; citations omitted.) You will fare no better – unless it is too blatant for the court to presume otherwise – if you fail to show abuse by presenting the lower court's reasoning and actions. If your client is unwilling to pay for a court reporter, you may have to consider whether it is worth doing so on your own. In any event, I would recommend that you put this in writing and obtain the client's consent, including an acknowledgment that they are in effect waiving their right to appeal, unless the court commits a legal error.

113 You are entitled to a written record of the proceedings.

Code of Civil Procedure section 269(a) requires that an official reporter "shall take down in shorthand all testimony, objections made, rulings of the court, exceptions taken, arraignments, pleas, sentences, arguments of the attorneys to the jury, and statements and remarks made and oral instructions given by the judge or other judicial officer, . . ." in a civil case "on the order of the court or at the request of a party." (Code Civ. Proc., § 269(a)(1).) Don't agree to waive the court reporter because you don't believe an issue will arise during these proceedings or you feel pressured to do so by the judge and/or opposing counsel.

114 Find out the court's policy on court reporters.

The clerk's office should post its local policy regarding when official court reporters are available, and in which departments the services of court reporters are not available. If the services of a court reporter are not available, a party may arrange for one to serve as an official pro tempore reporter. (Cal. Rules of Court, rule 2.956.)

115 It is your duty to make sure a court reporter will be present.

"When counsel has reason to anticipate that what is said at a hearing may be pertinent to a subsequent appeal he has a duty to insure that a court reporter is present. (See, e.g., 1 Cal. Civil Procedure During Trial (Cont.Ed.Bar 1982) §§ 11.11-11.12.) Failure to attend to this duty can be tantamount to a waiver of the right to appeal." (*In re Christina P.* (1985) 175 Cal.App.3d 115, 129.) As I mentioned above, if the client refuses to pay for these costs, you should get the client's acknowledgment in writing that he or she may be waiving the right to appeal. Otherwise, you may be committing malpractice, which will be confirmed for all the world to see in a written opinion by the court of appeal.

116 If there is no court reporter, then consider an agreed on or settled statement.

If you intend to appeal on a ground that requires the oral proceedings, you must either include a reporter's transcript, an agreed statement, or a settled statement. While I am aware that some courts rely on videotaped proceedings, I recommend having these transcribed to make it easier on the appellate court to review the proceedings. An agreed statement can include statements as to how the superior court decided the points to be raised on appeal. (Cal. Rules of Court, rule 8.134(a)(1).) I am not crazy about an agreed statement as it seems difficult to get attorneys to agree on what happened at trial, but agreed statements can be used if you have a small case, there was no court reporter present at trial, and the parties did not want to undertake the added expense of a court reporter. A settled statement may be used where the oral proceedings were not reported or cannot be transcribed and requires the participation (but not necessarily an agreement as to what happened) of the attorneys and the court. In the end, the trial court will decide what happened at trial by settling the statement. (Cal. Rules of Court, rule 8.137.)

117 Order a record of the closing argument.

In most cases, I recommend getting a complete reporter's transcript of the trial, including closing argument. Some attorneys dispense with closing argument. After all, it isn't evidence. However, it can serve several needs. First, I prefer to see how the attorneys, and by extension, the juries, view the record. It can act as a checklist for me as to the building blocks of your case. Second, you must have a transcription of the closing argument if you are claiming judicial or attorney misconduct during this phase of the trial. If it does not appear on the record, the reviewing court will presume no error occurred. (*Worthington Corp. v. El Chicote Ranch Properties, Ltd.* (1967) 255 Cal.App.2d 316, 320.)

II. Creating a Clear Record

118 Speak slowly and with clarity and precision.

Trial is that rare spectator sport that not only contemplates an oral presentation but a possible subsequent written transcription of the proceedings. A meaningful record should be clear, leaving nothing to the imagination. While I am in a position that I can ask a trial attorney what was meant by this question or answer, the court of appeal is not in the same position. You cannot sit next to a justice and offer explanations when the language isn't clear. You must speak with clarity and precision, and if the answer provided lacks clarity, then you must ask follow-up questions to ensure the answer is clear. Appearing in court usually produces anxiety, no matter how experienced we are as attorneys. As a result, we often speak faster and higher, and we may not even be aware that we are doing so. Learn how to control your voice to keep it slow and at an even tempo.

119 Read an old trial transcript to understand how you and others speak during trial.

As an exercise, find an old trial or law and motion transcript. Do you notice how *real* people speak in incomplete sentences and frequently use pronouns that can lead to confusion? Although it might sound redundant, avoid *this* or *that* as well as pronouns *he, she, it, they,* and *them*, when a more specific description may be provided. If the judge fails to complete a sentence or ruling, return to it as a follow-up question or summary before continuing on. I have experienced a number of interrupted rulings, and because of the nature of the discussion, the judge never returns to complete the ruling. It also is confusing when two names are discussed and then the thread continues with *she, he, her* or *him*. Also, avoid leaving references such as "here," "there," or "this long," etc., without more specific descriptions. If you are really interested in learning how you sound to others, you might even have a videotape or audiotape taken of one of your presentations.

120 Understand that your words maybe read by others not present at trial.

Trial lawyers are frequently surprised when they review the reporter's transcripts. What sounded like an eloquent argument can appear as a bunch of incomplete sentences that drift off without an ending. While trial lawyers may feel they are being clear *at trial,* this clarity may evaporate when the sole source of information is the written transcript. The reader cannot see that you are pointing to something or making gestures that enhance communication. You may want to imagine that your presentation is something that a reader or an appellate justice will only hear on the radio.

121 Make sure the testimony is audible.

In examining witnesses, make sure their responses are audible. Their response can get lost if others are also speaking at the same time or interrupting them. If a witness answers a question while the attorney is still speaking, make sure the answer appears on the record. Ask for some clarification or confirmation that the witness's answer is on the record or that you heard the witness correctly. Also clarify the record by indicating if the witness is nodding or making other gestures. If you are asking a witness to point to something, make sure the reader can understand what the witness intends. Again, if you keep in mind that readers will hear this as a radio broadcast, as suggested above, you will understand what you need to do to create an accurate picture for them.

122 Imagine how your words will be read.

This problem requires that the trial attorney step outside of the proceedings to some extent, and envision how such exchanges are viewed by a justice who is limited to reading a reporter's transcript. Perhaps it would be helpful to imagine the jurors or judge are blind; communicate in a way that aids them to visualize your case. Also remember that if you or another individual is using humor, sarcasm, anger, irritation, etc., the reader might not be able to pick up on these emotions.

123 Create a visual picture of the testimony.

When you hear an answer, think about how it will read on paper. If you ask the witness how far away he or she was, and you receive an answer that says something like "from here to there," try to get an estimate of the distance between the points. The same rule applies when the witness is pointing at something and then says "right here." Give detailed descriptions of demonstrations or visual evidence. Otherwise no one reading the transcript will know what you mean.

III. Get it all on the record!

124 Move exhibits into evidence.

Sometimes, in the midst of trial, attorneys introduce exhibits but fail to move them into evidence. Keep track of exhibits, including the numbers and letters assigned to them, and make sure you get them admitted into evidence. You may want to prepare a checklist of exhibits with a quick description of the exhibit, a column for its assigned number, and a column that indicates whether the exhibit was admitted into evidence. Always keep a copy of the exhibit, and if you are dealing with a large exhibit, make a reduced copy that can be included in the Clerk's Transcript. If you do not move exhibits into evidence, it may not be considered as part of the "evidence" introduced at trial. For instance, a deposition not offered and marked for identification may not be considered on appeal even though it was filed with the court below. (*Beverly Hills Nat'l. Bank v. Glynn* (1968) 267 Cal.App.2d 859, 866, fn. 1.) You may be able to cure this defect if all parties refer to the evidence and conduct themselves as if it were admitted. "The failure to formally and expressly offer the documents into evidence is not necessarily fatal, where the court and both parties treat the documents as if they were in evidence." (*Komas v. Future Systems, Inc.* (1977) 71 Cal.App.3d 809, 812; *Estate of Connolly* (1975) 48 Cal.3d 129, 132, fn. 4; *Walsh v. Walsh* (1952) 108 Cal.App.2d 575, 579.)

125 Exhibits are considered part of the record.

Exhibits are considered a part of the record, although they may not be transmitted to the court of appeal unless they are specifically designated. (Cal. Rules of Court, rule 8.122(a)(3).) However, where the appellant intends to rely on an exhibit, even to argue the exhibit should have been admitted or excluded, it is his or her duty to make sure the exhibit is transmitted to the appellate court. "Where exhibits are missing we will not presume they would undermine the judgment." (*Western Aggregates, Inc. v. County of Yuba* (2002) 101 Cal. App.4th 278, 291.)

126 Be precise when talking about exhibits.

Start with the number and a description of the exhibit, and continue to refer to the exhibit by number or document throughout the questioning. If you are reading a transcript or legal document, refer to page and line. Problems often arise when attorneys talk about the next exhibit in line, or jump from exhibit to exhibit, and I can't always tell which exhibit they are talking about.

127 Keep a copy of every exhibit, including the opposing party's exhibits.

This is a real source of problems for appellate attorneys. Trial attorneys often lose track of where the exhibits have gone after trial. Sometimes the exhibits are kept by the trial court, although the court may pressure the attorneys to take back the exhibits so that they do not clutter the court's exhibit room. Sometimes the exhibits are released to the party admitting them, and oddly enough, on occasions all exhibits have been released to one party. If you believe your case is going up on appeal, ask that the court maintain possession of them. Having a your own copy can help if you have to ask the appellate court to recognize a copy of the original exhibit but the best protection is to have the superior court maintain possession of exhibits so that the appellate attorney does not have to hunt them down and the courts have maintained a chain of custody to avoid any inference that the exhibits have been tampered with.

128 If you are dealing with diagrams, blow-ups, maps and charts, create an 8.5x11 reduction or an 8x10 photo.

These reductions will fit quite handily into the clerk's transcript or as appended material to a brief. You don't want the appellate court to wait until the very end to take a look at important exhibits. And if they are really important, such as a contract or report, then add the admitted exhibit as part of your appendix in the Appellant's Opening Brief, as permitted by California Rules of Court, rule 8.224(a)(3).)

129 Make sure there is a written transcript of electronic records.

Generally, the court reporter is not required to take down or transcribe an electronic recording admitted into evidence. (Cal. Rules of Court, rule 2.1040(b).) It is a better practice to obtain a written transcript for the convenience of the reviewing court. California Rules of Court, rule 2.1040(a) provides that "[u]nless otherwise ordered by the trial judge, a party offering into evidence an electronic sound or sound-and-video recording must tender to the court and to opposing parties a typewritten transcript of the electronic record. The transcript must be marked for identification. A duplicate of the transcript, as defined in Evidence Code section 260, must be filed by the clerk and must be part of the clerk's transcript in the event of an appeal. Any other recording transcript provided to the jury must also be marked for identification, and a duplicate must be filed by the clerk and made part of the clerk's transcript in the event of an appeal."

130 Don't forget to request judicial notice in writing, when appropriate, and obtain a ruling on your request.

Remember to prepare a written request for judicial notice, when appropriate, and obtain a ruling on it. (Evid. Code, § 453.) While appellate courts have the power to take judicial notice of matters that were not before the trial court, they will seldom do so absent "exceptional circumstances," especially when the party should have requested judicial notice below. "Reviewing courts generally do not take judicial notice of evidence not presented to the trial court. Rather, normally 'when reviewing the correctness of a trial court's judgment, an appellate court will consider only matters which were part of the record at the time the judgment was entered.' . . . No exceptional circumstances exist that would justify deviating from that rule, either by taking judicial notice or by exercising the power to take evidence under Code of Civil Procedure section 909." (*Vons Companies, Inc. v. Seabest Foods, Inc.* (1996) 14 Cal.4th 434, 444, fn. 3; *Franklin Mint Co. v. Manatt, Phelps & Phillips, LLP* (2010) 184 Cal. App.4th 313, 332, fn. 9.)

131 Remember that depositions and interrogatory answers are not automatically part of the record.

Depositions and interrogatory responses are not automatically part of the record, even if lodged with the trial court. They should be read into the record - with references to the pages and lines of testimony - or attached to an appropriate declaration.

IV. And finally . . .

132 Be nice to your court reporter!

Think of the court reporter as part of your team and try to make his or her life as easy as possible. That means spelling difficult names, speaking slowly and loudly, avoiding nodding or other gestures without speaking, and not speaking over each other. Be courteous and watch for visual cues as to the reporter's need for breaks. It will pay off in the long run!

~ Tips for Success ~

- Always request the presence of the court reporter for conferences when you believe important issues will be discussed.
- Get all objections and rulings made in sidebar and in-chambers conferences on the record, even if they are summarized after the fact.
- Think of the court reporter as part of your trial team.
- Create a clear and precise record by anticipating how readers will understand what happened at trial.
- Pay attention to how you speak and imagine that you are talking over the radio.
- Be considerate of the court reporter by spelling names, speaking clearly and without rushing so your words are understood, avoiding or describing gestures, and being alert to cues that the court reporter may need a break.

CHAPTER 7. COURT TRIALS: THE STATEMENT OF DECISION

An all too familiar scenario: *You waive a jury trial because you believe the judge can be fair in deciding your case. Despite your best efforts, the court rules against your client. You can't believe it! You want to appeal immediately even before the ink is dry on the judgment. You call your appellate attorney to get the appeal in motion. The appellate attorney asks, "Did you request a statement of decision?"*

You ponder the ramifications of this question and ask, "Was I supposed to? Can I still do it?"

On the other hand, if you had requested the statement of decision, you might tell the appellate attorney that it was inaccurate and failed to address all of your 48 requests, which more than covered all of the principal controverted issues in the case. The appellate attorney would then ask, "Did you object to the statement of decision?" You reply that you thought it would be futile as the judge had already made up his or her mind.

What is wrong with these answers?

133 Know the rules regarding statements of decisions.

Problems frequently arise in requesting, preparing, and objecting to the statement of decision. Attorneys who are facing a court trial would serve their clients' interests well by becoming familiar with the procedures involved in crafting this document. An obvious problem is failing to request findings on all material issues. Attorneys who customarily proceed with a jury trial may not be familiar with this process and are often not thinking about an appeal. They may also think that their job is done by making the request and that the record is preserved, but if they fail to object, it is as if the request was never made in the first place. (*In re Marriage of Arceneaux* (1990) 51 Cal.3d 1130, 1133-1134; Code Civ. Proc., § 634.) These errors may make an appeal more difficult and expensive, and may even result in the loss of an otherwise viable ground for appeal. (See Appendix A, Form Nos. 1-4, for sample forms related to statements of decisions.)

134 Understand the purposes of the statement of decision.

According to Code of Civil Procedure section 632, the statement of decision "explain[s] the factual and legal basis for [the trial court's] decision as to each of the principal controverted issues at trial . . ." A statement of decision is sufficient if "it fairly discloses the court's determination as to the ultimate facts and material issues in the case." (*Golden Eagle Ins. Co. v. Foremost Ins. Co.* (1993) 20 Cal. App.4th 1372, 1380.) It allows "the trial court to review its memorandum of intended decision and 'to make ... corrections, additions, or deletions it deems necessary or appropriate.' . . . Such statement thus enables a reviewing court 'to determine what [law] the trial court employed . . . .' It is the statement of decision which allows the court to place upon *the record* its view of facts and law of the case." (*In re Marriage of Ditto* (1988) 206 Cal.App.3d 643, 647; citations omitted.) In summary, the statement of decision serves several purposes:

- Protects against implied findings and presumptions;
- Allows the trial court to correct its intended decision, if warranted;
- Frames the issues for appeal; and
- Helps the appellate court conduct its review.

135 The statement of decision can be helpful for a number of reasons.

The statement of decision provides the court's reasoning and makes the case easily reviewable on appeal. If the trial court merely found for the defendant, no one could be sure whether the trial court's decision was based on the failure to establish one or more elements – and which ones – or the court's reliance on an affirmative defense. That would put the losing party in the position of appealing on all conceivable grounds and require the appellant to show that he or she had proven all elements of a cause of action and the winning party failed to prove all affirmative defenses. If you know the case is barred by the statute of limitations, you wouldn't want to spend time discussing duty, breach, causation or damages. And if you could demonstrate these elements were proven and the court's decision was later overturned on the statute of limitations defense, it would be important to know that you otherwise would have prevailed.

136 Before any hearing, find out if the court is required to issue a statement of decision upon request.

A trial court is not always required to issue a statement of decision, even after a timely request. For instance, the trial court is not required to issue a statement of decision in ruling on a motion (*Lavine v. Hospital of the Good Samaritan* (1985) 169 Cal.App.3d 1019, 1026), on an application for a preliminary injunction (*People v. Landlords Professional Services* (1986) 178 Cal.App.3d 68, 72), or where the only issue is a question of law. The appellate court can resolve legal issues without the benefit of the trial court's reasoning because these issues are reviewed de novo. (*TME Enterprises, Inc. v. Norwest Corp.* (2004) 124 Cal. App.4th 1021, 1030, but see *Gruendl v. Oewel Partnership, Inc.* (1997) 55 Cal.App.4th 654, 656, 660 [statement of decision required in hearing on motion to amend judgment to add alter ego liability].)

137 Make a proper request for statement of decision.

The request must "specify those controverted issues as to which the party is requesting a statement of decision." (Code Civ. Proc., § 632; Cal. Rules of Court, rule 3.1590 (d).) The court may direct a party to prepare the statement of decision or prepare it without the assistance of counsel. (Cal. Rules of Court, rule 3.1590(c).) It may also order that the tentative decision will be the statement of decision unless a party specifies controverted issues or makes additional proposals within 10 days. (Cal. Rules of Court, rule 3.1590(c)(4).) (See Appendix A, Form No. 1 for a sample "Request for Statement of Decision.")

138 Make a timely request for statement of decision.

After the court announces its tentative decision, a party may request a statement of decision. If the trial lasted less than one calendar day or took less than eight hours over more than one day, the request must be made *before* the matter is submitted for decision. (Cal. Rules of Court, rule 3.1590(n).) In all other cases, the request must be made within 10 days after the court announces its tentative decision. (Code Civ. Proc., § 632; Cal. Rules of Court, rule 3.1590(d).) That 10-day period is extended by five days pursuant to Code of Civil Procedure section 1013(a) where the court's tentative decision is served by mail. The court may extend the times prescribed by written order. (Cal. Rules of Court, rule 3.1590(g).) A party may also orally request a statement of decision. (*Whittington v. McKinney* (1991) 234 Cal.App.3d 123, 126; *In re Marriage of Ananeh-Firempong* (1990) 219 Cal. App.3d 272, 284.) (See Appendix A, Form No. 1, for a sample "Request for Statement of Decision.")

139 Don't use the request for statement of decision to attack the trial court.

Some requests for statement of decision may seek the trial court's reasoning on *every* issue – whether or not they are necessary to the judgment – and on every fact. While the trial court is required to make findings on "material subsidiary issues of fact," if they are requested (*Midwest Television, Inc. v. Scott, Lancaster, Mills & Altha, Inc.* (1988) 205 Cal.App.3d 442, 457), the trial court can limit the statement to those issues specified in the request, even if the parties have failed to specify all material issues. (Code Civ. Proc., § 632; *Harvard Investment Co. v. Gap Stores, Inc.* (1984) 156 Cal.App.3d 704, 709, fn. 3.)

140 Don't expect the court to address all subsidiary issues.

While each principal issue at trial should be addressed by the trial court, findings on subsidiary issues are not required. "The trial court need not discuss each question listed in a party's request; all that is required is an explanation of the factual and legal basis for the court's decision regarding the principal controverted issues at trial as are listed in the request." (*Hellman v. LaCumbre Golf & Country Club* (1994) 6 Cal.App.4th 1224, 1230.) "Only where a trial court fails to make findings as to a material issue which would fairly disclose the determination by the trial court would reversible error result." (*People v. Casa Blanca Convalescent Homes, Inc.* (1984) 159 Cal.App.3d 509, 524, abrogated on other grounds in *Cel-Tech Communications, Inc. v. Los Angeles Cellular Telephone Co.* (1999) 20 Cal.4th 163, 185-186.)

141 Don't use the request for statement of decision to interrogate the trial court.

Don't expect the trial court to respond individually to numerous requests. Although the request may require the trial court to specify the factual and legal bases for its decision, as noted above, it may not "interrogate the judge" on evidentiary matters. (*People v. Casa Blanca Convalescent Homes, Inc.* (1984) 159 Cal.App.3d 509, 525, abrogated on other grounds in *Cel-Tech Communications, Inc. v. Los Angeles Cellular Telephone Co.* (1999) 20 Cal.4th 163, 185-186 [appellant was conducting an inquisition by asking 75 questions].); *Onofrio v. Rice* (1997) 55 Cal.App.4th 413, 424-425 [defendants requested findings on 61 questions and argued the trial court erred in failing to make findings on 20 requests].) Some requests take on an argumentative tone or are obviously excessive. For example, a statement of decision that includes 75 separate requests usually suffers from these defects. No court wants to respond to numerous and unnecessary requests and may take the easy way out by refusing to be "interrogated" by a party. (*Kroupa v. Sunrise Ford* (1999) 77 Cal.App.4th 835, 842 [73 requests].) You will not have served your client's interests by preparing argumentative and voluminous requests. The trial court is not required to respond to every request made of it by a party. As stated in *Golden Eagle Ins. Co. v. Foremost Ins. Co.* (1993) 20 Cal. App.4th 1372:

> "The trial court is not required to respond point by point to the issues posed in a request for statement of decision. The court's statement of decision is sufficient if it fairly discloses the court's determination as to the ultimate facts and material issues in the case."

(*Id.* at pp. 1379-1380.) The trial court is not required to make findings with regard to detailed evidentiary facts and to make minute findings as to individual items of evidence. (*People v. Casa Blanca Convalescent Homes* (1984) 159 Cal.App.3d 509, 524, (abrogated on other grounds in *Cel-Tech Communications, Inc. v. Los Angeles Cellular Telephone Co.* (1999) 20 Cal.4th 163, 185-186.)

142 **Begin preparation of the statement of decision with a sorting process.**

Conceptualize the legal elements of the plaintiff's causes of action, organize and discuss the facts and the law supporting those elements. Since the statement of decision explains the factual and legal bases for the court's decision as to each principal controverted issue, you must first decide which issues are "principal controverted issues," and which ones are immaterial or tangential. This sorting process must be done with a goal in mind. If you intend to appeal, you must determine what issues are essential to support the judgment on appeal. "A 'material' issue of fact is one that is relevant and essential to the judgment and closely and directly related to the trial court's determination of the ultimate issue in the case.' [Citation.]" (*Midwest Television, Inc. v. Scott, Lancaster, Mills & Altha, Inc.* (1988) 205 Cal.App.3d 442, 457.) (See Appendix A. Form No. 3, for a sample "Proposed Statement of Decision.")

143 Distinguish between ultimate facts and conclusions of law that support the court's decision.

Another sorting process involves distinguishing between the factual and legal basis for the court's decision. This is not as easy as it sounds. The "factual basis" is even more refined; you must sort out ultimate facts from evidentiary facts, which need not be included in the statement of decision (*Ingredient Communication Council, Inc. v. Lungren* (1992) 2 Cal.App.4th 1480, 1497), because it is assumed findings on ultimate facts necessarily include the evidentiary facts necessary to sustain them. (*Murquiz v. City of Emeryville* (2000) 79 Cal. App.4th 1106, 1125.) Ultimate facts are deduced from evidentiary facts, resulting in a conclusion of fact. Attorneys often get confused with the distinction between an ultimate fact and a conclusion of law. As stated in *Hayward Lumber & Inv. Co. v. Construction Products Corp.* (1952) 110 Cal.App.2d 1:

> "The distinction between an ultimate fact and a conclusion of fact on the one hand, and a conclusion of law on the other, is not an easy one to draw. The finding of an ultimate fact usually, if not always, involves one or more conclusions. The rule which requires findings of facts does not require the finding of evidentiary facts but only that ultimate facts be found; it does not exclude conclusions of facts but only conclusions of law . . . . Whether a finding is one of an ultimate fact or a conclusion of law depends on the nature of the evidence. 'If,

> from the facts in evidence, the result can be reached by that process of natural reasoning adopted in the investigation of truth, it becomes an ultimate fact, to be found as such. If, on the other hand, resort must be had to the artificial processes of the law, in order to reach a final determination, the result is a conclusion of law.'"

(*Id.* at p. 3; citations omitted.) As stated in *Yield Dynamics, Inc. v. TEA Systems Corp.* (2007) 154 Cal.App.4th 547, 559, "'Ultimate fact[]' is a slippery term, but in general it refers to a core fact, such as an element of a claim or defense, without which the claim or defense must fail." The trial court's conclusion of law is its application of law to the facts. You want to pinpoint the trial court's reasoning so you are able to point out that the trial court misconstrued the law or facts. By doing so, you are giving the trial court an opportunity to correct its error. Use the Court's tentative decision as a guide, even if you disagree. A statement of decision should objectively reflect the court's reasoning. If you disagree, then make objections to the statement of decision.

144 Sort out ultimate facts from evidentiary facts.

If you are trying to sort out the ultimate facts from evidentiary ones, ask yourself "How is this conclusion supported?" For instance, a principal controverted issue may be whether your medical malpractice complaint is barred by the statute of limitations. The ultimate fact is that on a certain date plaintiff suspected her injury was caused by Dr. A's treatment. The question then becomes "Upon what facts could the court base its conclusion?" These facts may include plaintiff's visits to her physician, conversations with other consulting physicians, etc. These facts are evidentiary facts. Through a process of deduction – much like Sherlock Holmes – you have separated the ultimate facts from the evidentiary ones.

145 Prepare a comprehensive statement of decision so as to avoid the doctrine of "implied findings."

If you fail to determine the court's reasoning on factual determinations, your appeal will be bound by the doctrine of "implied findings," which means that all factual determinations are presumed in favor of the judgment. (*Marriage of Arceneaux* (1990) 51 Cal.3d 1130, 1133-1134.) "This doctrine requires that in the absence of a statement of decision, an appellate court will presume that the trial court made all factual findings necessary to support the judgment for which substantial evidence exists in the record. In other words, the necessary findings of ultimate facts will be implied and the only issue on appeal is whether the implied findings are supported by substantial evidence." (*Shaw v. County of Santa Cruz* (2008) 170 Cal. App.4th 229, 267.) Thus, if there was some conflict in the evidence, the reviewing court will presume the trial court believed the defendant. (See Appendix A, Form No. 3, for a sample "Proposed Statement of Decision.")

146 A timely and sufficient objection avoids the inference that the findings support the judgment.

A sufficient objection avoids the inference the findings in question support the judgment. (Code Civ. Proc., § 634; *In re Marriage of Arceneaux* (1990) 51 Cal.3d 1130, 1133.) If the statement does not resolve a controverted issue or is ambiguous, and counsel brought the omission or ambiguity to the trial court's attention, it may not be inferred on appeal, on a motion for new trial, or on a motion to vacate that "the trial court decided in favor of the prevailing party as to those facts or on that issue." (Code Civ. Proc., § 634.) (See Appendix A, Form No. 4, for a sample "Objections to Proposed Statement of Decision.")

147 The trial court is required to make separate findings on each category of damages.

The trial court is required upon request to make separate findings on general damages and the categories of special damages; however, it is not required to explain its computations or the process utilized. (*Gordon v. Wolfe* (1986) 179 Cal.App.3d 162, 167.) This requirement makes it easier for the parties to determine how the damages were allocated. Any other result would require a plaintiff to attack and support each category when the error might be only in one category, such as failing to include damages for loss of earning capacity. Suppose the plaintiff failed to request or object to the statement of decision, and thereafter, appealed the trial court's award. An appealing plaintiff could lose an appeal because the reviewing court would infer that the trial court made factual findings to support the judgment. Thus, while the trial court may have made an error by ignoring a category of damages, the reviewing court might simply infer there was no error and the trial court just reduced the damages sought consistent with the facts presented by defendant that the amount was excessive.

148 If appropriate, make proposals to the statement of decision.

If a party has requested a statement of decision, any other party can make proposals as to the content of the statement of decision within 10 days after the date of request for a statement of decision. (Cal. Rules of Court, rule 3.1590(e).) The statement of decision and proposed judgment must be prepared and mailed within 30 days after announcement or service of the tentative decision. (Cal. Rules of Court, rule 3.1590(f).) If the proposed statement of decision and judgment are not submitted or served within that 30-day period, then any other party may submit a proposed statement of decision and judgment or serve and file a motion within a 10-day period that the statement of decision be deemed. (Cal. Rules of Court, rule 3.1590(f).) (See Appendix A, Form No. 2, for a sample "Proposals to Content of Statement of Decision.")

149 If you don't agree with the statement of decision, file timely objections.

If you want to protect the record on appeal, it is not enough simply to request a statement of decision; you must also object to a proposed statement if it is inaccurate within 15 days after it has been served. (Cal. Rules of Court, rule 3.1590(g).) An objection to the statement of decision must be specific, rather than general, or else the issue will be deemed waived and will not be preserved for appellate review. "When a statement of decision does not resolve a controverted issue, or if the statement is ambiguous and the record shows that the omission or ambiguity was brought to the attention of the trial court either prior to entry of judgment or in conjunction with a motion under Section 657 or 663, it shall not be inferred on appeal or upon a motion under Section 657 or 663 that the trial court decided in favor of the prevailing party as to those facts or on that issue." (Code Civ. Proc., § 634; *Tusher v. Gabrielsen* (1998) 68 Cal. App.4th 131, 140-141.) (See Appendix A, Form No. 4, for a sample "Objections to Proposed Statement of Decision.")

150 Failing to object to defects in the statement of decision can hurt your appeal.

If a party fails to object to the statement of decision, that party may be deemed to have waived the right to object to the statement of decision on appeal. It is not enough to simply request a statement of decision; the Code of Civil Procedure outlines a two-step process: a request and an objection. (*In re Marriage of Arceneaux* (1990) 51 Cal.3d 1130, 1133-1134.) In *In re Marriage of Arceneaux,* the court stated:

> "[I]t would be unfair to allow counsel to lull the trial court and opposing counsel into believing the statement of decision was acceptable, and thereafter to take advantage of an error on appeal although it could have been corrected at trial."

(*Id.* at p. 1138.)

151 The court can order a hearing on the proposed statement of decision.

The court can order a hearing on the proposals and objections although it is not required to do so. (Cal. Rules of Court, rule 3.1590(k).) Some judges feel that by the time they have rendered their tentative decision, they have already heard enough argument and consider a hearing on the statement of decision, proposals, and objections as yet another opportunity to reargue the case without really focusing on the statement of decision. On the other hand, the losing party may view this hearing as another opportunity to show the defects in the court's decision, and quite possibly, change the court's mind.

152 A minute order is not a statement of decision.

The trial court cannot rely on a minute order to fulfill its duties under Code of Civil Procedure section 632, especially if it fails to explain the factual and legal bases for its decision as to the principal controverted issues at trial. (*Miramar Hotel Corp. v. Frank B. Hall & Co.* (1985) 163 Cal.App.3d 1126, 1129; *Whittington v. McKinney* (1991) 234 Cal.App.3d 123 [judgment reversed after trial court failed to issue a written statement of decision, concluding the oral proceedings and reporter's transcript would suffice].) However, courts often indicate that a tentative decision will become a statement of decision unless specifically requested. Such a statement allows the trial court to convert the tentative decision in a statement of decision. (*Slavin v. Borinstein* (1994) 25 Cal. App.4th 713, 718-719; see also California Rules of Court, rule 3.1590(c).)

153 A tentative decision or memorandum of decision is not a statement of decision.

A tentative decision or memorandum of decision is not a substitute for a formal statement of decision. "'A memorandum opinion is not a decision. Although it may purport to decide issues in the case, it is merely an informal statement of the views of the trial judge. It does not constitute findings of fact.'" (*Shaw v. County of Santa Cruz* (2008) 170 Cal. App.4th 229, 268 [applied the doctrine of implied findings when the appellant failed to request a statement of decision and relied on the trial court's "memorandum decision" to analyze its reasoning.] A tentative decision is not binding on the court nor can it be reviewed on appeal to determine the basis of the trial court's decision. (*Marriage of Ditto* (206 Cal.App.3d 643, 646-647.) In addition, a statement of reasons explains the court's ruling to the litigants, and not, as required in a statement of decision, to the court of appeal. (*Marriage of Buser* (1987) 190 Cal.App.3d 639, 642-643.) An explanation of the reasons for the court's ruling preserves the "integrity of adjudication" and the "fairness and effectiveness of adjudication are promoted by reasoned opinions." (*Nakamura v. Parker* (2007) 156 Cal.App.4th 327, 335-336.)

154 The court's refusal to prepare a statement of decision can work in favor of the losing party.

While the losing party has more to gain with a comprehensive statement of decision, the winning party should also want one. It will pin down the evidence and law, and if the loser fails to request one, the case will be bound by the doctrine of implied findings discussed above. There is another reason to obtain a statement of decision: if a timely request has been made for a statement of decision, but the trial court refuses to prepare one, it is reversible error. "Were we, conversely, to condone a total or even a material failure by trial courts to observe the prescribed procedure for revealing the basis for their respective decisions, we would be thrusting a quite substantial burden upon the litigants and also upon the appellate courts." (*Miramar Hotel Corp. v. Frank B. Hall & Co.* (1985) 163 Cal. App.3d 1126, 1129.) A reversal on this basis is seldom considered satisfactory because the case may be remanded for the issuance of the statement of decision, and thereafter, a party may file a new appeal. Of course, that means more time and expense. Reviewing courts also frown on a trial court's "short-hand method designed to avoid the mandate of section 632," such as an announcement by the court that the reporter's transcript contains the court's reasoning. "Any continued use of such procedures can only be construed as a refusal to comply with section 632, which will require a reversal." (*Whittington v. McKinney* (1991) 234 Cal.App.3d 123, 129.)

155 The trial court's failure to address damages may also result in reversible error.

The failure of the trial court to set out its computation of damages or the particular evidence it relied on also justifies a reversal per se. (*Gordon v. Wolfe* (1986) 179 Cal.App.3d 162, 167-168.) In that case, the plaintiff sought both general damages for pain and suffering and special damages for medical and incidental expenses, lost earnings, and lost earning capacity. The trial court gave its judgment in a lump sum figure. Because the damages were not broken down into categories, the reviewing court could not determine in what amount the award was intended to compensate plaintiff, thus "the judgment is effectively insulted from review by the substantial evidence rule." (*Id.* at pp. 167-168.) The appellate court acknowledged the trial court was not required to reveal the process by which it arrived at its figures; however, the appellate court could not determine what figure was assigned for each element of damages. It reversed the judgment and remanded the case to the trial court with directions to prepare a statement of decision.

156 An incomplete statement of decision will not necessarily result in a reversal.

If the statement is incomplete, but the judgment is supported by the evidence, it will not be reversed unless the "evidence is sufficient to sustain a finding in the complaining party's favor which would have the effect of countervailing or destroying other findings." (*Sperber v. Robinson* (1994) 26 Cal. App.4th 736, 745.) Essentially, an error in the statement of decision may be considered harmless if other findings in the statement are sufficient to support the judgment or the missing finding is implicit in other findings made by the trial court (*Wolfe v. Lipsy* (1985) 163 Cal.App.3d 633, 643-644), or when it is necessarily adverse to the appellant. (*Day v. Rosenthal* (1985) 170 Cal.App.3d 1125, 1162.)

157 (Maybe) all is not lost if you did not request a statement of decision.

Although it makes an appeal more difficult, the failure to obtain a statement of decision or object to a defective one does not necessarily destroy your client's appeal. For instance, you may still pursue an appeal despite the doctrine of implied findings if there is absolutely no evidence, or the court misconstrued the testimony, supporting a factual determination. However, if there is conflicting testimony on a material issue and the court finds against you, it may be presumed that your side's testimony was not credible. As stated in *Shaw v. County of Santa Cruz* (2008) 170 Cal.App.4th 229, 267, even if the doctrine of implied findings is applied as to ultimate facts, the appellant can pursue the appeal based on a challenge that the implied findings are not supported by substantiate evidence. In addition, the doctrine of implied findings will not be applied if there were omissions or ambiguities in the statement of decision's factual findings which were timely brought to the attention of the trial court. (*Fladaboe v. American Isuzu Motors Inc.* (2007) 150 Cal. App.4th 42, 59-60.)

158 You can still pursue your appeal if the error is simply one of law.

A statement of decision is not required for issues of law. (*Elysium Institute, Inc. v. County of Los Angeles* (1991) 232 Cal.App.3d 408, 421, fn. 2.) In a similar vein, you can still pursue an appeal without a statement of decision if the error of one of law. (*Von Klompenburg. v. Berghold* (2005) 126 Cal.App.4th 345, 348, fn. 3; *United Services Auto. Assn. v. Dalrymple* (1991) 232 Cal.App.3d 182, 186.) After all, such errors are reviewed on a de novo or independent standard of review.

159 Don't appeal from the statement of decision.

A statement of decision is generally not appealable. (*Industrial Indemnity Co. v. City and County of San Francisco* (1990) 218 Cal.App.3d 999, 1003, fn. 3.) Typically, the statement of decision precedes a formal order or judgment (*Grossman v. Davis* (1994) 28 Cal.App.4th 1833, 1836, fn. 1; *Industrial Indemnity, supra,* at p. 1003, fn. 3.); however, a reviewing court may treat the statement of decision as appealable when it apparently constitutes the court's final decision on the merits. (*Estate of Lock* (1981) 122 Cal.App.3d 892, 896; *Native Sun/Lyon Communities v. City of Escondido* (1993) 15 Cal.App.4th 892, 896, fn. 1.) (See Appendix D, Form No. 16 for a sample "Judgment after Bench Trial.")

~ Tips for Success ~

- After a bench trial, request a timely statement of decision on all principal controverted issues.
- Carefully tailor your request for a statement of decision; avoid excessive or argumentative requests, or requests on subsidiary issues.
- Request a statement of decision to segregate and allocate damages.
- Find out if a statement of decision is authorized in other types of hearings.
- If ordered by the court, prepare a comprehensive statement of decision, sorting the legal bases from the ultimate facts.
- Carefully review the statement of decision; make written proposals to add to it, and if appropriate, file a written objection.
- Understand why tentative decisions, memorandums of decision, and minute orders are not statements of decision.
- A statement of decision is not necessary to challenge legal errors.
- Don't appeal from the statement of decision; appeal from the judgment that follows.

CHAPTER 8. JURY TRIALS

An all too familiar scenario: *You prepared a special jury instruction that you wanted the court to give to the jury. During an in-chambers conference, the trial court rejects it, but there is no record of the ruling. The filed special jury instruction does not reflect whether the instruction was to be given or how the court ruled. You also prepared a special verdict form, but after talking to the jury, you discover the jurors were confused by the questions and reached inconsistent verdicts. You call your appellate attorney for help.*

What advice might you expect?

I. Jury instructions

160 Think about your jury instructions as you prepare for trial.

At trial, you will be required to prove your case to the jury, including the elements of each cause of action. The jury instructions contain those elements and will be used by the jury to determine if you have established your case. These jury instructions contain the law as these laypeople will come to apply it, and chances are that you know far more law than they do. In 2003, the Judicial Council California Civil Jury Instructions (CACI) were adopted in an attempt to be user-friendly to lay juries. Attorneys will often draft special instructions in addition to the standard instructions to deal with situations not adequately covered by CACI. Trial judges are understandably nervous about giving special instructions, especially since CACI offers so many tested instructions. They fear that special instructions increase the risk of instructional error and may open the door for an appeal, especially if the special instruction cites language from a case that is taken out of context or has a special application to the circumstances presented in another case. They also reason that if the party is relying on a statute, he or she may simply request judicial notice, and thus, there is no need for a special instruction for a statute. No matter whether you use preprinted or special instructions, give a lot of thought to your jury instructions and try to view them from the jury's perspective. (See Appendix B, Form Nos. 5-8, for sample forms related to jury instructions.)

161 Request jury instructions on each theory of your case.

"Each party in a civil proceeding must request complete and comprehensive instructions on its theory of the case; if a party fails to do so, the court ordinarily has no duty to instruct on its own motion." (*Bullock v. Phillip Morris USA, Inc.* (2008) 159 Cal. App.4th 655, 675.) On the other hand, "[a] party is not entitled to instructions with regard to a theory or defense that the party has *not advanced*." (*Boeken v. Philip Morris, Inc.* (2005) 127 Cal.App.4th 1640, 1672; italics in original.)

162 Make sure your jury instructions are clear and unambiguous.

When you prepare your jury instructions, make sure they are specific and clear. Check for contradictions and inconsistencies. You may want to read them to a layperson because your jury will probably be composed of laypeople. The trial court is under no duty to instruct on its own. "In a civil case, each of the parties must propose complete and comprehensive instructions in accordance with his theory of the litigation; if the parties do not do so, the court has no duty to instruct on its own motion." (*Downing v. Barrett Mobile Home Transport, Inc.* (1974) 38 Cal.App.3d 519, 523.) "A civil litigant must propose complete instructions in accordance with his or her theory of the litigation and a trial court is not 'obligated to seek out theories [a party] might have advanced, or to articulate for him that which he has left unspoken.'" (*Mesecher v. County of San Diego* (1992) 9 Cal. App.4th 1677, 1686; *Gagosian v. Burdick's Television & Appliances* (1967) 254 Cal.App.2d 316, 318 ["There is neither reason nor justification for compelling a trial judge to act as a sort of advisory or 'backup' counsel, with all the frustration of the employed attorneys' trial strategy and tactics which such a holding could encompass."].) "Neither a trial court nor a reviewing court in a civil action is obligated to seek out theories plaintiff might have advanced, or to articulate for him that which he has left unspoken." (*Finn v. G.D. Searle & Co.* (1984) 35 Cal.3d 691, 701-702.) Keep in mind; however, your instructions must be properly selected and framed. "'The trial court is not required to give instructions which are not correct statements of the law or are incomplete or misleading.'" (*Conservatorship of Gregory* (2000) 80 Cal.App.4th 514, 522.) (See Appendix B, Form Nos. 5-8, for sample forms related to jury instructions.)

163 Be timely in presenting your proposed jury instructions.

California Code of Civil Procedure section 607a requires that proposed jury instructions must be presented before the first witness is sworn. (See California Rules of Court, rule 2.1055 for the format for approved and special jury instructions.) Additional jury instructions may be proposed before argument "upon questions of law developed by the evidence and not disclosed by the pleadings." (Code Civ. Proc., § 607a.) Check local rules and find out if the judge has specific requirements for when and how jury instructions are proposed, although they should not conflict with California Rules of Court, rule 2.1055(e). In general, you should file a Request for Jury Instructions and an Index of Jury Instructions, which attaches all jury instructions. The form CACI instructions should be edited to fill in all blanks and pronoun references, and should delete unnecessary bracketed material. Include the CACI instruction number and title at the top of the paper. When you submit special instructions, number them consecutively and list the authority for the instruction on the bottom.

164 Make five sets of jury instructions.

I would recommend five sets of jury instructions for: you, opposing counsel, the trial judge, a copy to file with the clerk, and a copy you can mark up at conferences. Make sure you obtain a conformed filed copy. The conference to determine which jury instructions shall be given is usually not reported, so after the conference, you should take steps to memorialize the parties' positions and the court's rulings, especially if your proposed instructions are rejected. You will also want to get on the record the fact that the opposing parties may have agreed to withdraw or abandoned their proposed instructions, or conceded their instructions were unnecessary. If the court modifies any instruction you have proposed, make a record to show whether you objected or agreed to the modification. Make sure the jury instructions are accurate, and object if they are not.

165 Make sure the trial judge rules on the jury instructions.

California Rules of Court, rule 2.1055 requires that each set of jury instructions include an index. The Index should include a checklist so that the trial court may simply check whether the instruction was given as proposed, modified, refused or withdrawn If the record fails to indicate whether an instruction was refused, withdrawn, abandoned, or lost, the reviewing court will presume the appellant withdrew the instruction. "'[I]t is incumbent upon . . . appellant . . . to make certain that the trial court has ruled [on a requested instruction] and that the record on appeal discloses that ruling before the alleged ruling may be assigned as error." (*Bullock v. Philip Morris USA, Inc.* (2008) 159 Cal.App.4th 655, 678; citations omitted.) A trial court is under no duty to modify or edit an instruction. If the instruction is incomplete or erroneous, the trial judge may properly refuse it. (*Boeken v. Philip Morris, Inc.* (2005) 127 Cal.App.4th 1640, 1673.)

166 Try to get the reason(s) for the court's rejection of a proposed jury instruction on the record.

In *Bullock v. Philip Morris USA, Inc.* (2008) 159 Cal.App.4th 655, the appellate court noted that the reasons for rejecting a proposed instruction did not appear on the record because the conference on jury instructions was held in chambers and was not reported. There was no final set of jury instructions that included refused instructions. Although the attorney who represented Philip Morris indicated it would file a document showing the refused jury instruction, the document filed did not identify any refused instructions nor did Philip Morris raise the argument in its new trial motion. The court noted there were possible explanations for the rejection, i.e., "the instruction was improper, that one or both parties withdrew its request for the instruction and objected to the instruction during the unrecorded conference, that the parties or the court concluded that the instruction was unnecessary, or that the court or the party who prepared the final set of instructions simply overlooked the requested instruction and mistakenly omitted it." (*Id.* at p. 678.) No matter what the reason was, that ground for appeal was lost because the party could not show that the trial court actually rejected the instruction. While you should try to get the court's reasons for rejecting an instruction on the record immediately after the rejection is made, you may be able to raise this rejection and get it on the record as part of your motion for new trial.

167 If you plan to appeal based on the erroneous admission or rejection of a jury instruction, you must show who proposed it.

Make sure the record shows who prepared or requested the jury verdict form, otherwise your appeal might be subject to waiver or invited error. If you proposed the erroneous jury instruction and it was given, then you might have invited the error and waived any right to challenge it on appeal (*Faulk v. Soberanes* (1961) 56 Cal.2d 466, 471.) As a consequence, the appellant may not complain about an instruction that he or she has requested. (*Mayes v. Bryan* (2006) 139 Cal.App.4th 1075, 1090.) When the record fails to show who requested a jury instruction, the reviewing court will presume the instruction was given at the appellant's request. (*Lynch v. Birdwell* (1955) 44 Cal.2d 839, 847-848.) "It is, of course, plaintiff's burden, as appellant, to present a record which is sufficiently complete to establish that the claimed errors were not invited by him, and in the absence of such a showing he may not properly complain." (*Phillips v. Noble* (1958) 50 Cal.2d 163, 169.) Moreover, if the rejection is not on the record, the reviewing court will presume the instruction was withdrawn. (*Huber, Hunt & Nichols, Inc. v. Moore* (1977) 67 Cal. App.3d 278, 312.)

168 Make the rejected jury instruction part of the record.

Attorneys and judges frequently go over jury instructions in the judge's chambers. These conferences are often unreported, even though instructional error is often raised on appeal. The parties may go over a stack of instructions and the judge must decide if each is to be given as prepared, modified, rejected, or withdrawn. Written instructions must be submitted pursuant to Code of Civil Procedure section 607a, and the court "on request of counsel, must: (1) decide whether to give, refuse, or modify the proposed instructions; (2) decide which instructions shall be given in addition to those proposed, if any; and (3) advise counsel of all instructions to be given." (Code Civ. Proc., § 607a.) If the trial court refuses to give an instruction, it still must be made part of the record; otherwise, the error is waived. (*Gaspar v. Georgia Pacific Corp.* (1967) 248 Cal. App.2d 249, 251.)

169 Jury instructions should be identified by a number and should indicate the party requesting the instruction or whether it was given by the court on its own motion, refused, modified or withdrawn.

The trial court should indicate whether the instruction was given, refused, or given as modified, with the modification clearly indicated. (*Lynch v. Birdwell* (1955) 44 Cal.2d 839, 846.)

170 Know the standards of review applicable to jury instructions.

In determining whether a jury instruction should have been given, the appellate court will assume that the jury might have believed the evidence upon which the instruction was predicated, and if a correct instruction had been given, the jury might have rendered a verdict in favor of the losing party. (*Henderson v. Harnischfeger Corp.* (1974) 12 Cal.3d 663, 674.) Instructional error is deemed prejudicial when it seems probable that the error prejudicially affected the verdict. (*Green v. State of California* (2007) 42 Cal.4th 254, 267.) "'Article VI, section 13 of the California Constitution provides that error in instructing the jury shall be grounds for reversal only when the reviewing court, 'after an examination of the entire cause, including the evidence,' concludes that the error 'has resulted in a miscarriage of justice.' The test of reversible error has been stated in terms of the likelihood that the improper instruction misled the jury. [Citation.]'. . . . Thus, if a review of the entire record demonstrates that the improper instruction was so likely to have misled the jury as to become a factor in the verdict, it is prejudicial and a ground for reversal. . . . 'To put it another way, 'where it seems probable that the jury's verdict may have been based on the erroneous instruction prejudice appears and this court 'should not speculate upon the basis of the verdict.''' (*Mock v. Michigan Millers Mutual Ins. Co.* (1992) 4 Cal. App.4th 306, 335; citations omitted.)

171 Object to instructional error or the issue may be waived on appeal.

The failure to object to instructional error may be waived if it is not raised at the trial court below. But see *Mock v. Michigan Millers Mutual Ins. Co.* 4 Cal. App.4th 306, 333 [appellant objected to one of two instructions; however, "given the manifest error of these two instructions, especially when considered together," further objections were not required]. In addition, according to Code of Civil Procedure section 647, errors related to giving an instruction, refusing to give one, or modifying the instruction are deemed excepted to; however, if the instruction is argued to be too general or incomplete, the appellant may have waived this ground unless he or she requested an additional or qualifying instruction. The court in *Suman v. BMW of North America, Inc.* (1994) 23 Cal. App.4th 1 pointed out the difference:

> "When a trial court gives a jury instruction which is correct as far as it goes but which is too general or is incomplete for the state of the evidence, a failure to request an additional or a qualifying instruction will waive a party's right to later complain on appeal about the instruction which was given. (*Mock v. Michigan Millers Mutual Ins. Co.* (1992) 4 Cal. App.4th 306, 333-334 [5 Cal.Rptr.2d 594].) However, when a trial court gives a jury instruction which is prejudicially *erroneous as given,* i.e., which is an incorrect statement of law, the party harmed by that instruction need not have objected to the instruction or proposed a correct instruction of his own in order to preserve the right to complain of the erroneous instruction on appeal."

(*Id.* at p. 9.) Given the pressures of trying cases, you may not necessarily know whether the instruction is too general or constitutes an incorrect statement of law. You should object in either situation.

172 Challenge the trial court's failure to instruct.

You may not be able to attack the trial court's failure to instruct unless you have proposed an instruction on the issue (*Agarwal v. Johnson* (1979) 25 Cal.3d 932, 950-951, disapproved on other grounds in *White v. Ultramar* (1999) 21 Cal.4th 563, 574, fn. 4.), and the proposed instruction is a correct statement of the law. In *Wank v. Richman & Garrett* (1985) 165 Cal.App.3d 1103, the court held the trial court may reject an erroneous, misleading or incomplete instruction and is under no duty to modify an instruction once the jury is properly instructed as to the law of the case. There are two exceptions that may arise if the judge (1) fails to instruct on a material issue and a controlling legal principle (*Paverud v. Niagara Machine & Tool Works* (1987) 189 Cal.App.3d 858, 863, overruled in part by *Soule v. General Motors Corp.* (1994) 8 Cal.4th 548) or (2) the trial could modify the instruction so that it becomes a correct statement of the law. (*Wank v. Richman & Garrett, supra,* at p. 1114.)

173 Consider the factors in establishing prejudicial error.

In *Mock v. Michigan Millers Mutual Ins. Co.* (1992) 4 Cal.App.4th 306, the appellate court noted that to determine whether the probable effect of an instruction has been to mislead the jury requires consideration of all of the circumstances of the case, including the evidence and other instructions given. The court rejected any finding that a precise formula can be drawn. Instead, it focused on two factors "(1) the degree of conflict in the evidence on critical issues and (2) the effect of other instructions in remedying the error." (*Id.* at p. 335.) The court cited *LeMons v. Regents of University of California* (1978) 21 Cal.3d 869, which outlined five factors: "(1) the degree of conflict in the evidence on critical issues . . . ; (2) whether respondent's argument to the jury may have contributed to the instruction's misleading effect . . . (3) whether the jury requested a rereading of the erroneous instruction . . . or of related evidence . . . ; (4) the closeness of the jury's verdict . . . ; and (5) the effect of other instructions in remedying the error. . .'" (*Id.* at p. 876; citations omitted.) (See also *Soule v. General Motors Corp.* (1994) 8 Cal.4th 548, 580-581.)

II. General and special verdicts

174 Use CACI forms as a guide in preparing verdict forms.

CACI includes proposed jury verdict forms for many causes of action. You may want or even need to break down the damages that the jury can award. This breakdown can serve as a reminder of what damages are requested. You may also want to distinguish between non-economic and economic damages, further breaking economic damages into various categories. This breakdown may be more helpful in obtaining a higher verdict because the jury's attention is drawn to the separate damage categories rather than arriving at a single figure. As noted in *Greer v. Buzgheia* (2006) 141 Cal.App.4th 1150, 1159, the model verdict forms contained in the Judicial Council of California Civil Jury Instructions are intended as models and may need to be modified to fit the facts of the case. (See Appendix C, Form Nos. 9-15, for sample forms related to verdict forms.)

If punitive damages are sought, a general verdict with special interrogatories or a special verdict form must be used to allow the jury to make special findings on this issue and separating the compensatory from punitive damages. (Code of Civil Procedure section 625; *Myers Building Industries, Ltd. v. Interface Technology, Inc.* (1993) 13 Cal.App.4th 949.) In medical malpractice actions under the Medical Injury Compensation Reform Act (MICRA), the verdict form must include special findings on compensation for future damages. (Code Civil Proc., § 667.7.) When the defendant seeks an offset for damages attributable to another person's fault, a general verdict must also allocate between certain non-economic damages pursuant to Proposition 51. (Civil Code, § 1431.2.) (See Appendix C, Form No. 15, for a sample "Verdict with Special Findings re Punitive Damages." Appendix D, Form Nos. 17-19, includes sample forms for judgments after jury trials, using general verdicts, general verdicts with special interrogatories, and special verdict forms.)

175 A general verdict is more easily affirmed on appeal.

A general verdict is favored in uncomplicated cases because it leaves fewer decisions for the jury to make and there is less of a possibility of confusing the jurors. General verdicts are more easily affirmed on appeal. Because a general verdict is not broken down as to the issues, it implies findings on all issues favorable to the winning party. (*Myers Building Industries, Ltd. v. Interface Technology* (2003) 13 Cal. App.4th 949, 959.) (See Appendix C, Form Nos. 9-12, for sample general verdict forms.)

Pursuant to Code of Civil Procedure section 624, the general verdict "is that by which [the jury] pronounce[s] generally upon all or any of the issues, either in favor of the plaintiff or defendant; . . ." To affirm the judgment, the prevailing party can rely on a theory that is free from prejudicial error and supported by substantial evidence. Even when several causes of action are tried and a general verdict is given for the plaintiff, the appellate court assumes the jury found on the theory supported by substantial evidence and free from error. "'Where several counts or issues are tried, a general verdict will not be disturbed by an appellate court if a single one of such counts or issues is supported by substantial evidence and is unaffected by error, although another is also submitted to the jury without any evidence to support it and with instructions inviting a verdict upon it . . .' This rule assumes that the jury found on the cause of action or theory which was supported by substantial evidence and as to which there was no error." (*McCloud v. Roy Riegels Chemicals* (1971) 20 Cal.App.3d 928, 935-936; *Gillespie v. Rawlings* (1957) 49 Cal.2d 359, 369.)

Conversely, when the verdict is in favor of the defense, it implies a finding in the defendant's favor on any defense theories supported by the evidence. (*McCloud v. Roy Riegels Chemicals, supra,* at pp. 935-936.) Thus, even if the jury voted for your client on an erroneous theory, the mistake will not be apparent on appeal. You may also consider whether to prepare a general verdict for each cause of action if multiple causes of action are alleged. Needless to say, plaintiffs often prefer general verdicts, while defendants prefer a general verdict with special interrogatories.

176 Consider a general verdict with interrogatories.

A general verdict with interrogatories is a cross between the general and the special verdict, which requires the jury to make findings on the ultimate facts of the case, leaving the judgment to the trial court. A general verdict with interrogatories tests the validity of the general verdict. "The purpose of special interrogatories is to test the validity of the general verdict by determining whether all facts essential to the verdict were established to the satisfaction of the jury. No party has a right to submission of special interrogatories." (*Hurlbut v. Sonora Community Hosp.* (1989) 207 Cal.App.3d 388, 403.) According to Code of Civil Procedure section 625, the court may direct the jury to render a general verdict and to "find upon particular questions of fact, to be stated in writing, and may direct a written finding thereon." (See Appendix C, Form No. 12, for a sample "General Verdict with Special Findings.")

If a general verdict is inconsistent with the special findings of fact, the special findings of fact control over the general verdict and judgment should be entered accordingly. (*Tavaglione v. Billings* (1993) 4 Cal.4th 1150, 1155; Code Civ. Proc., §625.) "The law is well settled that, '[a] special finding is inconsistent with the general verdict only when, as a matter of law, the special finding when taken by itself would authorize a judgment different from that which the general verdict will permit.' Since the special verdict or finding provided for in [Code Civ. Proc.,] section 625 is '. . . primarily and principally for the purpose of determining whether the general verdict is or is not against law' no presumption is to be indulged in favor of answers to special interrogatories and every reasonable intendment in favor of the general verdict is indulged." (*Wyler v. Feuer* (1978) 85 Cal.App.3d 392, 404.) Other factors affecting the decision to use this type of verdict are (1) it may highlight specific issues, (2) it can educate the jury, and (3) it can isolate critical issues. It can also address and preserve specific issues for appeal. (*Heiner v. Kmart Corp.* (2000) 84 Cal.App.4th 335, 346.)

177 Make a timely request for special findings.

California Rules of Court, rule 3.1580 provides that "Whenever a party desires special findings by a jury, the party must, before argument, unless otherwise ordered, present to the judge in writing the issues or questions of fact on which the findings are requested."

178 Segregate your request for damages.

Damages should be segregated. As noted above, there are situations where damages must be segregated. If they are not, it may be impossible to argue the jury failed to award damages for specific types of damages, such as medical specials or loss of future earnings. (*Moore v. Preventive Medicine Group* (1986) 178 Cal.App.3d 728, 746-747.) "'Unfortunately, appellant did not seek a segregation of the elements of damages from the jury, and the jury was not required to do so without such request.'" (*English v. Lin* (1994) 26 Cal.App.4th 1358, 1368-1369, citing from *Enriquez v. Smyth* (1985) 173 Cal. App.3d 691, 700.) "To preserve for appeal a challenge to separate components of a plaintiff's damage award, a defendant must request a special verdict form that segregates the elements of damages." (*Greer v. Buzgheia* (2006) 141 Cal.App.4th 1150, 1158 [verdict form too general to preserve a reduction claim under *Hanif/Nishihama*].) The failure to request that the jury segregate elements of damages may result in a waiver when it cannot be ascertained how the jury distributed damages or if it awarded damages for certain claims. (*Moore v. Preventive Med. Medical Group, supra,* at pp. 745-746.) (See Appendix C, Form No. 14, for a sample breakdown of damages.)

179 Watch out for the possibility of inconsistent verdicts.

A special verdict is seldom used because of the potential problems that can arise. A special verdict is one where the jury finds the facts only, leaving the judgment to the trial court. It presents the ultimate facts in the case, which must be resolved by the jury so that nothing else remains except for the court's conclusions of law. "The requirement that the jury must resolve every controverted issue is one of the recognized pitfalls of special verdicts. 'The possibility of a defective or incomplete special verdict, or possibly no verdict at all, is much greater than with a general verdict that is tested by special findings. . . .'" (*Myers Building Industries, Ltd. v. Interface Technology, Inc.* (1993) 13 Cal.App.4th 949, 959; *Falls v. Superior Court* (1987) 194 Cal. App.3d 851, 854-855.)

There is always a chance of inconsistent verdicts if you use a special verdict form. Jurors can be confused by too many detailed questions. Using a special verdict increases the chances of an inconsistent verdict where the requests are ambiguous and inconsistent. "By its nature, a special verdict has 'recognized pitfalls' because it requires the jury to resolve all controverted issues in a case, unlike a general verdict which implies findings on all issues in a party's favor." (*Oxford v. Foster Wheeler LLC* (2009) 177 Cal.App.4th 700, 707.) If the verdict is ambiguous, the appellant should request a more formal and certain verdict. The judge can send the jury out with proper instructions to correct the insufficient verdict. If the jury has been discharged before the objection is raised, the trial court must then interpret the verdict after considering the pleadings, evidence and instructions. The appellate court will then attempt to give a correct interpretation, but if the verdict is hopelessly ambiguous, the judgment must be reversed. "If the verdict is merely ambiguous, a party's failure to request a correction or clarification of the verdict before the jury is discharged may amount to a waiver of the ambiguity or defect, particularly if the party's failure to object was to reap a 'technical advantage' or to engage in a 'litigious strategy.'" (*Zagami, Inc. v. James A. Crone, Inc.* (2008) 160 Cal.App.4th 1083, 1092, fn. 5; *Mizel v. City of Santa Monica* (2001) 93 Cal.App.4th 1059, 1070-1071; Code Civ. Proc. § 619; But see *Lambert v. General Motors* (1998) 67 Cal.App.4th 1179, 1182 [no objection was required to preserve the issue for review pursuant to Code Civ. Proc. § 619].)

180 Object to an erroneous verdict form.

You should review the verdict form for potential problems, such as the possibility of inconsistent findings, and if necessary, object at trial. If the appellant fails to do so, the appellate court will find the appellant has waived any objection to the verdict form. (*Green v. Rancho Santa Margarita Mortgage Co.* (1994) 28 Cal.App.4th 686, 696; *Lynch v. Birdwell* (1955) 44 Cal.2d 839, 851; see also *Pacific Construction, Inc. v. City of Sunnyvale* (2007) 155 Cal.App.4th 525, 550-551 [failure to object in trial court to special verdict form on specific ground asserted on appeal forfeited claim of error]; *Mardirossian & Associates, Inc. v. Ersoff* (2007) 153 Cal.App.4th 257, 277 ["Because [appellant] did not challenge the special verdict form on this ground below, we do not consider it for the first time on appeal"].) You can request that the special verdict be modified (*John Y. v. Chaparral Treatment Center, Inc.* (2002) 101 Cal.App.4th 565, 579-580), include additional matters (*Wilson v. Ritto* (2003) 105 Cal.App.4th 361, 366-367), or you may also object to the specific verdict form on such grounds that it is insufficient. (*Heppler v. J.M. Peters Co.* (1999) 73 Cal. App.4th 1265, 1287.)

III. Bad Behavior During Trial

A. Misconduct by opposing counsel

181 Object when opposing counsel's misconduct creates prejudice or appeals to the jury's sympathies, shock or horror.

Opposing counsel's attempts to appeal to the sympathies of the jurors or to show that a party was calloused and inhumane, are prejudicial and are intended to play upon the jury's emotions of sympathy, shock and horror. These are improper matters for the jury to consider and should be objected to as soon as possible. "The sum result of counsel's remarks was such as to create an atmosphere of bias and prejudice which manifestly was calculated to deprive defendant of a fair trial. Certainly such conduct cannot be condoned. However we are nevertheless persuaded to the conclusion that defendant has waived its right to complain by its failure to make timely objections, . . ." (*Horn v. Atchison, T. & S. F. R. Co.* (1964) 61 Cal.2d 602, 609-610.)

182 Object to the opposing party's request that the jury award damages as if they or a loved one were the injured party.

You should object if the plaintiff's attorney asks the jurors to put themselves in the place of the injured plaintiff. It is improper to appeal to the jury to fix damages as if they or a loved one were the injured plaintiff. In *Horn v. Atchison, T. & S. F. R. Co.* (1964) 61 Cal.2d 602, the court cited from *Zibbell v. Southern Pacific Co.* (1911) 160 Cal. 237, 255: "'"It is, of course, improper for the jury to attempt to measure the damage occasioned by the injury and the sufferings attendant upon it, by asking themselves what sum they would take to endure what plaintiff has endured, and must endure . . . 'No rational being would change places with the injured man for an amount of gold that would fill the room of the court, yet no lawyer would contend that such is the legal measure of damages.'" (*Id.* at p. 609.)

183 Make specific objections to opposing counsel's misconduct.

Object to misconduct by opposing counsel and request a curative admonition. "Generally a claim of misconduct is entitled to no consideration on appeal unless the record shows a timely and proper objection and a request that the jury be admonished." (*Horn v. Atchison, T. & S. F. R. Co.* (1964) 61 Cal.2d 602, 610.) Moreover, the court noted the rule is "remedial in nature, and seeks to give the court the opportunity to admonish the jury, instruct counsel and forestall the accumulation of prejudice by repeating improprieties, thus avoiding the necessity of a retrial." (*Ibid.*) The court in *Horn* observed that the attorney for the defendant was an experienced trial attorney and did not interrupt either the opening or closing arguments to make objections; on the contrary, he elected to sit by, waiting until the conclusion of closing argument, and then moved for a mistrial. The reviewing court also noted that it was only in "extreme cases" that an instruction by the trial court to the jury to disregard the misconduct will not correct the misconduct and remove its damaging affect. (*Ibid.*) In *Whitfield v. Roth* (1974) 10 Cal.3d 874, the court also noted that the error will be waived "'unless the misconduct was of so aggravated a character that it could not be cured by any instruction.'" (*Id.* at p. 892.)

184 Renew your objection to a rephrasing of the prejudicial argument.

After you have objected to opposing counsel's closing argument, you should renew the objection if opposing counsel rephrases the closing argument, which still contains the same improper argument. Failure to do so will result in a waiver. (*Sand v. Mahan* (1967) 248 Cal. App.2d 679, 689-690.)

B. Jury misconduct

185 In deciding whether the jurors have committed misconduct, distinguish between their mental processes and affirmative misconduct.

When jury misconduct is shown, it raises a rebuttable presumption of prejudice. (*In re Hamilton* (1999) 20 Cal.4th 273, 295.) "This presumption may be rebutted only by 'an affirmative evidentiary showing that prejudice does not exist or by a reviewing court's examination of the entire record to determine whether there is a reasonable probability of actual harm to the complaining party resulting from the misconduct.'" (*Glage v. Hawes Firearms Co.* (1990) 226 Cal.App.3d 314, 321.)

Before moving for new trial on the grounds of jury misconduct, make sure the mistake relates to affirmative misconduct, and not the subjective reasoning processes of the jury. "Declarations which impugn the jury's mental processes or the jurors' reasons for assenting to the verdict or attempt to show 'that the jury made no findings as to certain matters' are inadmissible under Evidence Code section 1150." (*Gorman v. Leftwich* (1990) 218 Cal.App.3d 141, 146.) This principle is based on the policy in favor of ensuring the stability of verdicts and protecting jurors against harassment. "Section 1150, subdivision (a) [of the Evidence Code], draws a distinction between proof of overt acts, objectively ascertainable, and proof of the subjective reasoning process of the individual juror, which can be neither corroborated nor disproved . . .' We noted that Evidence Code section 1150 limits impeachment evidence to 'proof of overt conduct, conditions, events, and statements . . . This limitation prevents one juror from upsetting a verdict of the whole jury by impugning his own or his fellow jurors' mental processes or reasons for assent or dissent. The only improper influences that may be proved under section 1150 to impeach a verdict, therefore, are those open to sign, hearing, and the other senses and thus subject to corroboration." (*Hasson v. Ford Motor Company* (1982) 32 Cal.3d 388, 413.) Evidence Code section 1150(a) provides:

> "Upon an inquiry as to the validity of a verdict, any otherwise admissible evidence may be received as to statements made, or conduct, conditions, or events occurring, either within or without the jury room, of such a character as is likely to have influenced the verdict improperly. No evidence is admissible to show the effect of such statement, conduct, condition, or event upon a juror either in influencing him to assent to or dissent from the verdict or concerning the mental processes by which it was determined."

In *In re Hamilton* (1999) 20 Cal.4th 273, the court examined the definition of "juror misconduct": "When the overt event is a direct violation of the oaths, duties, and admonitions imposed on actual or prospective jurors, such as when a juror conceals bias on voir dire, consciously receives outside information, discusses the case with nonjurors, or shares improperly information with other jurors, . . ." (*Id.* at pp. 294-295.) It may also include attempts by nonjurors to tamper with the jury, use of bribery, or intimidation. Other misconduct can include (1) conducting experiments to give the jury evidence not offered at trial (*Wagner v. Doulton* (1908) 112 Cal.App.3d 945, 950), (2) an individual juror conducting experiments at home (*Lankster v. Alpha Beta Co.* (1993) 15 Cal. App.4th 678, 682), (3) improper communications (*Iwekaogwu v. City of Los Angeles* (1999) 75 Cal.App.4th 803, 818), (4) reaching a quotient verdict by averaging all damage figures (*Chronakis v. Windsor* (1993) 14 Cal.App.4th 1058, 1066), and increasing personal injury awards to include attorney's fees. (*Krouse v. Graham* (1977) 19 Cal.3d 59, 81.)

186 Object to jury misconduct when jurors agree to disregard instructions.

To show jury misconduct, the moving party must submit declarations that show the jurors affirmatively agreed to disregard the instructions given. (*Gorman v. Leftwich* (1990) 218 Cal.App.3d 141, 146.) Jury misconduct may give rise to a presumption of prejudice, but that presumption can be rebutted. Any declarations submitted on this ground must show both *misconduct* and *influence over the jury's decision.* For example, it's not enough to show that the jury deliberately received information outside of the evidence presented at trial, you must also show that such information adversely influenced the jury's decision.

187 You cannot object to jury misconduct for the first time on appeal.

The appellate court takes a dim view of appellants who have knowledge of an opposing party's misconduct and yet wait until the verdict comes in before objecting. When the verdict turns out to be unfavorable, then and only then do they complain. "'"The defendant cannot be allowed to remain quiet and take the chances upon a favorable verdict, and then raise a point that he knew of and could have raised during the progress of the trial.' . . . 'Failure to object to the misconduct of jurors as soon as knowledge thereof is obtained and opportunity to object is presented is a waiver of the right to object, and the objection cannot be thereafter presented, as by a motion for a new trial."' (*Zibbell v. Southern Pacific Co.* (1911) 160 Cal. 237, 254.)

C. Judicial misconduct

188 Object to judicial misconduct that taints the trial.

Judicial misconduct, as opposed to judicial error, can occur when the trial court demonstrates bias or unfairness toward one of the parties. (*Haluck v. Ricoh Electronics, Inc.* (2007) 151 Cal.App.4th 994, 1008.) When a judge's conduct is inconsistent with recognized principles of judicial decorum "consistent with the presentation of a case in an atmosphere of fairness and impartiality," it may be deemed prejudicial, justifying a reversal. (*Id.* at 1002.) In *Haluck,* the court stated that "'The trial of a case should not only be fair in fact, . . . it should also appear to be fair.' The judge's actions and comments during trial violated these principles such that 'it shocks the judicial instinct to allow the judgment to stand."' (*Id.* at p. 1002.) The court in *Haluck* also found judicial misconduct when the trial court engaged in ex parte contacts with one of the lawyers and that the trial court violated its duties of judicial decorum and courtesy. (*Id.* at p. 1003.) It concluded that "This conduct was a sideshow in the overall circus atmosphere mocking a serious proceeding important to the parties, and it 'cast the judicial system itself in a bad light in the eyes of the litigants and the public at large.'" (*Id.* at p. 1004.) Judicial misconduct may also be shown when the judge makes discourteous and disparaging remarks to one attorney so as to discredit that attorney, create the impression that it is allying itself with the other attorney or the trial court makes statements that show it does not believe a witness's testimony. (*People v. Sturm* (2006) 37 Cal.4th 1218, 1233.)

189 The court of appeal will not find this ground waived if a request for a curative instruction would have been futile.

While an appellant may waive his or her objection to judicial misconduct by failing to object or ask for a curative instruction below, this ground will not be waived if the objection is deemed futile. (*Haluck v. Ricoh Electronics, Inc.* (2007) 151 Cal.App.4th 994, 1004.) "However, a defendant's failure to object does not preclude review 'when an objection and an admonition could not cure the prejudice caused by' such misconduct, or when objecting would be futile." (*People v. Sturm* (2006) 37 Cal.4th 1218, 1237.)

~ Tips for Success ~

- Propose complete and timely jury instructions that cover all of the theories of your case.
- Read your proposed jury instructions to laypersons to ensure they are clear and unambiguous.
- Check with the trial court to determine if it has special rules and policies regarding jury instructions and verdicts.
- Make sure all jury instructions are indexed and edited to eliminate blanks, brackets, and language that does not apply to the case.
- Make sure the record shows who proposed a jury instruction and the court's ruling on it.
- Object to instructional error or a failure to instruct.
- Object to problems with the verdict form.
- Object to misconduct by the court, opposing counsel, or the jury as soon as you are aware of it.
- Make a record of the jury's misconduct by post-trial motion(s).

CHAPTER 9. AFTER THE TRIAL IS OVER

An all too familiar scenario: *Trial is over and you didn't get the result you expected. The clients want to know why their "great" case was lost. They are talking about an appeal, all the way up to the U.S. Supreme Court, but they haven't even offered to pay what they owe you! You have told them you don't handle appeals and you have advised them that they need to find an appellate lawyer. Frankly, you want them out of your life because they don't seem to appreciate the hard work and money you have put into the case. You tell them to search for an appellate attorney in the Yellow Pages or through the Internet.*

Is this good advice?

190 Your job is not over because the trial ended.

If you are unsuccessful at trial, clients generally want to know why. They may feel that the judge was unfair or that the opposing counsel stooped to new lows. They may even threaten to take the matter "all the way up to the Supreme Court." Your job is not over simply because the trial ended, especially if the client has lost. You should advise the client as to what steps he or she should take once the decision is known. Litigation involves perseverance and stamina. A litigant may not win every battle and may lose before succeeding on appeal. Some clients may have to quit to preserve their sanity and emotional well-being. They may also face paying a judgment and costs, or when losing their appeal, they may end up paying the other side's attorneys fees and costs, adding considerably to the expense of litigation. Not every client can handle such expenses, and not every fight needs to be fought until the bitter end.

191 If you think there is going to be an appeal, urge the trial court to retain possession of the exhibits.

At the conclusion of trial, the trial court often urges the parties to pick up their exhibits. You should politely refuse to do so, requesting that the court maintain possession and custody of all exhibits. Because courts are becoming overburdened with files and exhibits, they try to avoid this responsibility, but it will avoid problems later if the court retains the exhibits. If the trial court maintains the exhibits, at least the parties know where the exhibits are and that no one has access to them to try to alter them without consent. It also makes it easier to transmit the originals to the court of appeal when required. (Cal. Rules of Court, rule 8.224.)

192 If the judgment is not automatically stayed on appeal, ask the trial court to stay enforcement of judgment until the notice of appeal can be filed and a bond obtained.

While some types of judgments or orders are automatically stayed on appeal, a money judgment is not automatically stayed. (Code Civ. Proc., § 917.1(a)(1).) It is important that your client understand that a money judgment can be typically enforced as soon as judgment is entered. Even if the client has a meritorious appeal, they may be crippled from going forward because the judgment is being enforced. They may not be in a position to pay the judgment or incur more attorney's fees to litigate enforcement proceedings. At the last hearing before judgment is entered, ask the trial court for a temporary stay pursuant to Code of Civil Procedure section 918. It is more cost effective to ask now rather than adding to the client's expenses by having the request made by ex parte application after judgment. The temporary stay may be granted to allow the client to decide whether or not to appeal and, if necessary and possible, to arrange for a bond.

193 Check your retainer agreement to ascertain if it covers post-trial motions or an appeal.

If your client is successful and you have won a monetary award, you may be motivated to stay with the case, but that feeling may not exist if you have lost and invested a substantial amount of time and expense in trying the case. If you choose not to become involved in the appeal, notify your client in writing, and if necessary, be sure to follow proper procedural steps in withdrawing from the case. This is especially true if execution on the judgment is not stayed and enforcement proceedings will be pursued. If you stay on and associate in an appellate attorney, make sure you get the client's written consent. Fee-sharing agreements must be in writing. (Rules Pro. Conduct, rule 2-200.) For example, in medical malpractice cases, the clients may not be charged more for associate counsel than the statutory limits on attorneys' fees for such cases. (Bus. & Prof. Code, § 6146; *Yates v. Law Offices of Samuel Shore* (1991) 229 Cal.App.3d 583, 591-592.) At a minimum, you may want to help the client by obtaining recommendations or at least pointing the client to groups that might provide referrals, such as local or state bar associations.

194 Inform your client *in writing* about the deadline for filing a notice of appeal.

If a client came to you for a consultation at the beginning of the case, you would certainly advise the client as to the applicable statute of limitations. So why not at the end of the case? It is simply not enough to mention this statutory deadline in a meeting, especially an emotional one. Put it in writing! You should also be sure to discuss how this deadline is affected by post-trial motions. (Cal. Rules of Court, rule 8.108.) Moreover, advise your client not to wait until the last minute to decide whether to appeal a judgment. Appellate attorneys customarily want to review the transcripts and may want a substantial retainer before agreeing to handle the appeal. I have observed situations where the trial attorney was stuck filing the notice of appeal because the client was unable to obtain new counsel in time.

195 If you are facing a deadline, file the notice of appeal in the name of the client.

"'If a judgment or order is appealable, an aggrieved party *must* file a *timely* appeal or forever *lose* the opportunity to obtain appellate review.'" (*Maughan v. Google Technology, Inc.* 143 Cal.App.4th 1242,

1247; *Norman I. Krug Real Estate Investments, Inc. v. Praszker* (1990) 220 Cal.App.3d 35, 46.) A timely notice of appeal is required to obtain jurisdiction; once the deadline has expired, the appellate court has no power to entertain the appeal. (*Van Beurden Ins. Servs., Inc. v. Customized Worldwide Weather Ins. Agency* (1997) 15 Cal.4th 51, 56.) If your client wants to appeal and has not found an appellate attorney, you may have to file the notice of appeal to protect yourself. Although the notice of appeal can be signed by the attorney with the client's consent pursuant to California Rules of Court, rule 8.100(a)(1), you may file the notice of appeal on behalf of the client in pro per. Thus, you will not be considered the attorney of record for the client at the appellate level.

196 Tell your client about the realistic chances of success and the costs of an appeal.

The truth of the matter is that most appeals are not successful for the simple reason that the court of appeal presumes judgments to be correct and is not anxious to send back cases for retrial. Errors often occur during trial, but they must be reversible errors resulting in a miscarriage of justice to merit a reversal or retrial. (California Constitution, article VI, § 13; Code Civ. Proc., § 475.) Typically, reversals are granted in 15-25% of cases. Be realistic about the costs of appeal. Discuss the financial implications of an appeal. In some circumstances when attorney's fees have been awarded against the appellant, a losing appeal may mean the appellant will end up paying the costs and attorneys on appeal for both sides. Moreover, a reversal may not be an absolute win, but can result in a retrial, which only adds to the appellant's costs and expenses.

197 Know when a motion for new trial or other post-trial motion must be made to preserve a challenge on appeal.

If you believe the damages awarded are inadequate or excessive, or you believe there is jury misconduct, then you must file a post-trial motion as a condition to raising the issue on appeal. "A failure to timely move for a new trial ordinarily precludes a party from complaining on appeal that the damages awarded were either excessive or inadequate, whether the case was tried by a jury or by the court." (*Jamison v. Jamison* (2008) 164 Cal.App.4th 714, 719-720; *Schroeder v. Auto Driveaway Co.* (1974) 11 Cal.3d 908, 918.) (See *Glendale Fed. Sav. & Loan Assn. v. Marina View Heights Development Co.* (1977) 66 Cal.App.3d 101, 122 ["The failure to move for a new trial, however, does not preclude a party from urging legal errors in the trial of the damage issue such as erroneous rulings on admissibility of evidence, errors in jury instructions, or failure to apply the proper legal measure of damages"].)

In *Glendale Fed. Sav. & Loan Assn. v. Marina View Heights Development Co., supra,* the court explained:

> "The rule is a sound one. The trial court is in a better position than a reviewing court to determine whether a jury verdict was influenced by passion or prejudice. Moreover, the power to weigh the evidence and resolve issues of credibility is vested in the trial court, not the reviewing court . . . Consequently, where the ascertainment of the amount of damage requires resolution of conflicts in the evidence or depends on the credibility of witnesses, the award may not be challenged for inadequacy or excessiveness for the first time on appeal. To permit a party to do so without a motion for new trial could unnecessarily burden reviewing courts with issues which can and should be resolved at the trial court level."

(*Id.* at p. 122; citations omitted.)

A motion for new trial is usually required before appeal in cases of jury misconduct because the grounds for such motions are often not known until after the trial is concluded and the jurors are interviewed. Thus, the motion for new trial may present the earliest opportunity to raise this ground and the only opportunity to get the facts of jury misconduct on the record. However, the attorney is required to show that neither the attorney nor the client were aware of the misbehavior until after the verdict was returned, furthermore, that such misconduct was promptly brought to the attention of the court. (*Weathers v. Kaiser Foundation Hospitals* (1971) 5 Cal.3d 98, 103.)

198 If judgment is entered or about to be entered, forget a motion for reconsideration.

While there is authority to the effect that the time for filing an appeal is extended by the service and filing of a valid motion for reconsideration of an "appealable order" under Code of Civil Procedure section 1008(a), there is no extension for filing an invalid motion. (Cal. Rules of Court, rule 8.108(e); *Branner v. Regents of Univ. of Calif.* (2009) 175 Cal.App.4th 1043, 1047-1048.) More importantly, there is no extension of time for filing a motion to reconsider the judgment; the proper remedy is a motion for new trial or to vacate. (*Ramon v. Aerospace Corp.* (1996) 50 Cal.App.4th 1233, 1236-1238; *Safeco Ins. Co. of Ill. v. Architectural Facades Unlimited, Inc.* (2005) 134 Cal.App.4th 1477, 1481.) While there may be some conflict in the cases on this point, the better approach is not to rely on the motion for reconsideration to extend the time for filing a notice of appeal. On rare occasions and on a showing of good cause, the trial courts have treated such motions as motions for new trial, but don't rely on the court do so. "If the record clearly indicates that the parties and the trial court ignored the label and treated the motion as one for new trial or to vacate the judgment, good cause might exist for this court to also ignore the label." (*Passavanti v. Williams* (1990) 225 Cal.App.3d 1602, 1610-1611; *20th Century Ins. Co. v. Superior Court* (2001) 90 Cal.App.4th 1247, 1259-1261.)

199 An invalid or untimely post-trial motion will not extend the time to file a notice of appeal.

A timely motion for new trial can extend the time for filing a notice of appeal for another 30 days, but no more than 180 days overall, where the motion is denied. (Cal. Rules of Court, rule 8.108(b).) The extension period is calculated from the earliest of: 30 days after the superior court clerk mails or a party serves an order denying the motion or notice of entry of that order, 30 days after denial of the motion by operation of law, or 180 days after entry of judgment. (Cal. Rules of Court, rule 8.108(b).) If the trial court fails to rule on the motion during the 60-day period after notice of entry of the judgment or after filing of the first notice of intention to move for new trial, the motion will be deemed denied by operation of law and the 30-day period runs from that date. (Cal. Rules of Court, rule 8.108(b)(1)(B).) The extensions by mail under Code of Civil Procedure section 1013(a) do not apply. (*Westrec Marina Management, Inc. v. Jardine Ins. Brokers Orange County, Inc.* (2000) 85 Cal.App.4th 1042, 1047-1049.) However, there is no extension of the 30-day period for an invalid motion for new trial. (Cal. Rules of Court, rule 8.108(b); Code Civ. Proc., § 659; *Ramirez v. Moran* (1988) 201 Cal. App.3d 431, 435-437.) The extension rules also apply to motions to vacate, but again the motion must be timely and based on recognized grounds (Cal. Rules of Court, rule 8.108(c).) It also applies to motions for judgment notwithstanding the verdict (JNOV), but again, the motion must be timely and valid. (Cal. Rules of Court, rule 8.108(d)(1).) (See Appendix E, Form No. 21, for a sample "Notice of Intention to Move for New Trial.")

200 Recognize when the time starts running to file a notice of appeal.

The filing deadlines for a notice of appeal are set forth in California Rules of Court, rule 8.104(a): (1) 60 days after service of notice of entry of judgment under rule 8.104(a)(2), (2) 60 days after the clerk's notice of entry of judgment under rule 8.104(a)(1), and (3) 180 days after entry of judgment. (The time period may be shorter for limited jurisdiction appeals as provided in California Rules of Court, rule 8.222(a).) I assume that in most cases the winning party will want to give notice of entry of judgment to lop off 120 extra days to think about filing the notice, so I calendar the case for 60 days after judgment is entered. By picking the shortest time period possible, I will never be late. There is some authority to the effect that the 60-day period starts to run even if the appellant never received notice of entry of judgment. (*Sharp v. Union Pac. R. R. Co.* (1992) 8 Cal.App.4th 357, 360.) Also, if my client is the appellant, he or she usually does not want to wait 180 days to get the appeal rolling. Also note that this deadline is not extended even if the notice of entry of judgment is served by mail, express or overnight delivery, or fax. (Cal. Rules of Court, rule 8.104(b).) If the last day falls on a legal holiday or weekend, then the deadline is extended to the next day the court is open. (Code Civ. Proc., §§ 12, 12a, 12b; Cal. Rules of Court, rule 8.60(a).)

201 Be aware of what constitutes notice of entry of judgment.

Pursuant to California Rules of Court, rule 8.104, the period of time for filing a notice of appeal can be cut down from 180 days to 60 by giving notice of entry of judgment. Sounds simple, but there is no document entitled "Notice of Entry" or "Notice of Entry of Judgment." Attorneys will often prepare such a document and attach a copy of the executed judgment. Beware that a file-stamped, executed copy of the judgment and proof of service, without any other document referencing its entry, is the same as giving notice of entry of judgment under California Rules of Court, rules 8.104(a)(1) and (2). The service of a conformed judgment can present a trap for the unwary because the time has started to run but meanwhile the attorney is waiting for a document entitled "Notice of Entry of Judgment." (*Alan v. American Honda Motor Co., Inc.*(2007) 40 Cal.4th 894, 905; Cal. Rules of Court, rules 8.104(a)(1) and (2).) (See Appendix D, Form No. 20, for a sample "Notice of Entry of Judgment.)

202 **Avoid filing a premature notice of appeal.**

It's not unusual for a lawyer to file a notice of appeal before it is required. The trial attorney is nervous about losing sight of the deadline and may believe it is better to file the notice earlier rather than later. This situation occurs when the attorney files a notice of appeal from an intended decision, statement of decision, a minute order that orders preparation of a written order, an order granting summary judgment, or an order sustaining a demurrer without leave to amend. A notice of appeal filed before entry of judgment may still be valid but courts have grown increasingly reluctant to save premature appeals or notices filed from the wrong document. (Cal. Rules of Court, rule 8.104(e); *Marriage of Battenburg* (1994) 28 Cal. App.4th 1338, 1341, fn. 1; *Cabral v. Soares* (2007) 157 Cal.App.4th 1234, 1239, fn 2.) You may have to make a motion for relief, asking the appellate court to construe the notice of appeal as being filed from the correct appealable judgment or order, or you may have to refile the notice of appeal to remedy the problem. Check the most current cases to determine how particular courts view and treat premature notices of appeal or appeals from non-appealable documents (while knowing that an appealable judgment or order is almost certainly to follow). (See Appendix D, Form Nos. 16-19, for sample judgment forms.)

203 Contact the reporter about the reporter's transcript.

To enable the client to make an informed decision about filing an appeal, you should ask for an estimate of the cost to obtain the reporter's transcripts. Sometimes these costs can be very expensive and may even affect the client's decision to go forward with the appeal. A cost estimate can also avoid tying up the client's funds. For instance, if the client files a notice designating the reporter's transcript as part of the record on appeal - which must be filed within 10 days after filing the notice of appeal - the client will be required to deposit the cost of the transcript at the time of the designation. (Cal. Rules of Court, rule 8.130(b).) If the costs are unknown, a deposit of $325 for hearings under three hours and $650 for hearings over three hours may be required. The actual cost of the transcript could be far less, so by obtaining a written cost estimate in advance or entering into a private arrangement with the court reporter (by paying the reporter and filing a waiver of the deposit in court), less money will be tied up and will be available for other costs. (Cal. Rules of Court, rule 8.130(b).) You may also deposit the estimated amount directly with the court. (Cal. Rules of Court, rule 8.130(b)(1)(A).)

204 File a timely notice of appeal.

The filing of a notice of appeal is jurisdictional. If you fail to file the notice of appeal with the superior court clerk in a timely manner, then the court of appeal has no authority to consider the appeal. "The time for appealing a judgment is jurisdictional; once the deadline expires, the appellate court has no power to entertain the appeal." (*Van Beurden Ins. Services, Inc. v. Customized Worldwide Weather Ins. Agency, Inc.* (1997) 15 Cal.4th 51, 56; *Janis v. California State Lottery Commission* (1998) 68 Cal.App.4th 824, 828-829.) Thus, if you have done everything right to preserve the record but your notice of appeal is late, then the appeal is pretty much dead. You cannot obtain relief under Code of Civil Procedure section 473(b) or by arguing party consent, stipulation, estoppel or waiver. (Cal. Rules of Court, rules 8.60(d) and 8.104(b).) Untimely appeals are subject to dismissal even if the respondent fails to make an objection or motion to dismiss. (*Maughan v. Google Technology, Inc.* (2006) 143 Cal.App.4th 1242, 1247.) (Untimely criminal appeals may be saved by the "constructive filing" doctrine, which is not discussed here.) There are rare, very rare, exceptions to this rule. By filing a timely notice of appeal, you have preserved your clients' rights - whether you are the attorney of record or they are listed as in pro per - so that the case is ready to turn over to the appellate specialist to work his or her magic! (Notices of Appeal can can be obtained in preprinted form, usually from the particular Court of Appeal's web site.)

~ Tips for Success ~

- If you think there might be an appeal, ask the trial court to retain possession of the trial exhibits.
- Notify your clients in writing of the statutory deadline for filing a notice of appeal - whether or not you think they want to appeal.
- If a motion for new trial must be brought as a condition to an appeal on specific grounds, you will probably have to do it.
- Revise your retainer agreement to indicate whether you handle appeals, and if so, that they will be subject to a separate written retainer agreement.
- Always find out if the judgment is automatically stayed on appeal or a bond is required to stay enforcement of the judgment.
- At the last hearing, ask the trial court for a temporary stay, up to 10 days after the notice of appeal is due, so your clients have time to arrange for a bond.
- If necessary, file a notice of appeal in your client's name in pro per to avoid losing their right to appeal.
- An appeal involves a financial decision; discuss the pro's and con's of an appeal as well as settlement options to ensure your client makes an informed choice.

Appendices

(*Note:* These forms are intended to be examples. Check with CACI for forms that are tailored to specific causes of action.)

Appendix A

Forms for Statement of Decision

Form 1: Sample Request for Statement of Decision

[*Name of attorney with Bar number*]
[*Address*]
[*Telephone*]
[*Fax number*]
[*E-mail, if appropriate*]

Attorney for [*Party*] [*name*]

SUPERIOR COURT OF CALIFORNIA

COUNTY OF __________

______________________,	)	CASE NO. ______________
	)	
Plaintiff,	)	Assigned for all purposes to:
	)	Judge [*name*]
vs.	)	Dept. No. ____
	)	
______________________,	)	**REQUEST FOR**
	)	**STATEMENT OF DECISION**
Defendant.	)	
	)	Complaint filed:
__________________________________	)	Trial date:

TO: [*Party*] [*name*] and [*his/her/its*] attorney of record, [*name*]:

[*Party*] [*name*] requests that, pursuant to Code of Civil Procedure section 632, the Court issue a Statement of Decision in this case. [*Party*] requests that the Statement of Decision explain the factual and legal bases for the Court's decision on each of the following controverted issues:

1. [*List issues, i.e., that the defendant breached the contract, or whether defendant breached a duty of care owed to plaintiff*]

2. Whether plaintiff's claimed medical expenses were reasonable

DATED: ___________

BY__________________________
[*Attorney's name*]
Attorney for [*Party*] [*name*]

Form 2. Sample Proposals to Content of Statement of Decision

[*Name of attorney with Bar number*]
[*Address*]
[*Telephone*]
[*Fax number*]
[*E-mail, if appropriate*]

Attorney for [*Party*] [*name*]

SUPERIOR COURT OF CALIFORNIA

COUNTY OF ___________

________________________,	)	CASE NO. _______________
	)	
Plaintiff,	)	Assigned for all purposes to:
	)	Judge [name]
vs.	)	Dept. No. ____
	)	
________________________,	)	**PROPOSALS TO CONTENT OF**
	)	**STATEMENT OF DECISION**
Defendant.	)	
	)	Complaint filed:
____________________________________	)	Trial date:

[*Party*] [*name*] makes the following proposals to the content of the Statement of Decision:

1. That the factual and legal bases for the Court's decision regarding the controverted issue of breach of contract should be explained as follows:

a. The Court based its decision on the following facts: [*Describe the facts that explain court's decision*].

b. The legal basis for the Court's decision is: [*Describe the legal determinations that explain the trial court's decision*]

DATED: ____________

Respectfully submitted,

BY___________________________
[*Attorney's name*]
Attorney for [*Party*] [*name*]

Form 3. Sample Proposed Statement of Decision

[*Name of attorney with Bar number*]
[*Address*]
[*Telephone*]
[*Fax number*]
[*E-mail, if appropriate*]

Attorney for [*Party*] [*name*]

SUPERIOR COURT OF CALIFORNIA

COUNTY OF __________

______________________,	)	CASE NO. _______________
	)	
Plaintiff,	)	Assigned for all purposes to:
	)	Judge [*name*]
vs.	)	Dept. No. ____
	)	
______________________,	)	**PROPOSED STATEMENT**
	)	**OF DECISION**
Defendant.	)	
	)	Complaint filed:
________________________________	)	Trial date:

This cause came on regularly for trial on [date], in Department No. ___ of the above-entitled Court, the Honorable [*name*], Judge Presiding, sitting without a jury. The parties waived a jury trial. Plaintiff, [*name*], appeared by [*his/her/its*] attorney, [*name*]. Defendant, [*name*], appeared by [*his/her/its*] attorney, [*name*].

Oral and documentary evidence was introduced on half of the parties. The cause was argued and submitted to the Court for decision. The Court, having considered the evidence and heard the arguments of counsel, and being fully advised, now issues the following Statement of Decision:

1. **Breach of contract:** On the issue of breach of contract, the Court's decision is as follows: [*describe the court's decision on this issue.*]

a. The Court based its decision on the following facts: [*describe the factual determinations that explain the court's decision*].

b. The legal basis for the Court's decision is [*describe the legal grounds for the court's decision*].

As a consequence of the above findings, judgment is hereby ordered to be entered as follows: [*describe court's judgment*].

DATED: ____________

BY____________________________

[*Attorney's name*]
Attorney for [*Party*] [*name*]

Form 4. Sample Objections to Proposed Statement of Decision

[*Name of attorney with Bar number*]
[*Address*]
[*Telephone*]
[*Fax number*]
[*E-mail, if appropriate*]

Attorney for [*Party*] [*name*]

SUPERIOR COURT OF CALIFORNIA

COUNTY OF __________

______________________,	)	CASE NO. ______________
	)	
Plaintiff,	)	Assigned for all purposes to:
	)	Judge [*name*]
vs.	)	Dept. No. ____
	)	
______________________,	)	**OBJECTIONS TO PROPOSED**
	)	**STATEMENT OF DECISION**
Defendant.	)	
	)	Complaint filed:
________________________________	)	Trial date:

[*Party*] [*name*] objects to the proposed Statement of Decision, prepared for the Court by [*party*] [*name*], as follows:

1. [*Party*] objects to the proposed Statement of Decision as to the statement of the factual basis for the court's decision as to Issue No. 1. [*Party's*] objection is based on the following grounds:

a. The statement of decision contains "facts" that do not accurately reflect the evidence presented at trial;

b. In its [*statement of decision* or *tentative decision*], the court indicated that . . .

2. [*Party*] objects to the proposed Statement of Decision because the Court has failed to explain the factual and legal bases for the Court's decision on each of the following controverted issues:

1. [*List issues, i.e., that the defendant breached the contract*];
2.
3.

DATED: ___________

BY___________________________
[*Attorney's name*]
Attorney for [*Party*] [*name*]

Appendix B

Forms for Jury Instructions

Form 5. Sample Request for Jury Instructions

[*Name of attorney with Bar number*]
[*Address*]
[*Telephone*]
[*Fax number*]
[*E-mail, if appropriate*]

Attorney for [*Party*] [*name*]

SUPERIOR COURT OF CALIFORNIA

COUNTY OF ___________

<table>
<tr><td>________________________,

Plaintiff,

vs.

____________________,

Defendant.

___________________________________</td><td>)
)
)
)
)
)
)
)
)
)
)</td><td>CASE NO. _______________

Assigned for all purposes to:
Judge [name]
Dept. No. ____

REQUEST FOR
JURY INSTRUCTIONS

Complaint filed:
Trial date:</td></tr>
</table>

TO: [*Party*] [*name*] and [*his/her/its*] attorney of record, [*name*]:

[*Party*] [*name*] respectfully requests that attached Instructions be given to the jury in the trial of this matter.

OR

[*Party*] [*name*] respectfully request that this Court give the following CACI Jury Instructions, as well as any additional instructions requested hereafter.

DATED: ____________

BY___________________________
[*Attorney's name*]
Attorney for [*Party*] [*name*]

Form 6. Sample Index of Proposed Instructions

[*Party's*] proposed jury instructions are indexed below. [*Party*] [*name*] has included this Checklist so that the Court may indicated if the Instruction was given as proposed, given as modified, refused, or withdrawn.

I. Approved Jury Instructions:

CACI No. ____

A. Given as requested: ______________

B. Given as modified: ______________

C. Refused: ______________________

D. Withdrawn: __________________

CACI No. ____

A. Given as requested: ______________

B. Given as modified: ______________

C. Refused: ______________________

D. Withdrawn: __________________

II. Proposed Special Jury Instructions:

Proposed Special Jury Instruction No. ____

A. Given as requested: ______________

B. Given as modified: ______________

C. Refused: ______________________

D. Withdrawn: __________________

Proposed Special Jury Instruction No. ____

A. Given as requested: ______________

B. Given as modified: ______________

C. Refused: ______________________

D. Withdrawn: __________________

Form 7. Sample CACI Form of Proposed Jury Instruction

CACI. No. ____

[*Quote text of CACI instruction.*]

***ADD*:**

1. Exact copy of CACI No. ___

OR

2. Exact copy of CACI No. ___, except adaptions.

OR

3. CACI No. ____, as modified.

GIVEN AS REQUESTED: ________

GIVEN AS MODIFIED: __________

REFUSED: ____________________

WITHDRAWN: _________________

DATED: ___________

BY_________________________
Judge of Superior Court

(***Note*:** Pursuant to California Rules of Court, rule 2.1055(c)(3), prepare jury instruction without any blank lines or unused bracketed portions.)

Form 8. Sample CACI Form of Special Jury Instruction

Special Jury Instruction No. ____

[*Text of special instruction*]

GIVEN AS REQUESTED: ________

GIVEN AS MODIFIED: __________

REFUSED: ____________________

WITHDRAWN: ________________

DATED: ___________

BY_________________________
Judge of Superior Court

Authorities:

(As required by California Rules of Court, rule 2.1050(e).)

Appendix C

Forms for General and Special Verdicts

Form 9. Sample General Verdict

From CACI No. VF-5000 - General Verdict Form - Single Plaintiff - Single Defendant - Single Cause of Action.

SUPERIOR COURT OF CALIFORNIA

COUNTY OF ___________

________________________,	) CASE NO. _______________
	)
Plaintiff,	) Assigned for all purposes to:
	) Judge [*name*]
vs.	) Dept. No. ____
	)
________________________,	) **GENERAL VERDICT**
	)
Defendant.	)
	)
____________________________________	)

We, the jury in the above-entitled action, having determined our general verdict, find as follows:

Select one of the following two options:

_____ We find in favor of plaintiff [*name*] and against defendant [*name*] and award damages to plaintiff [*name*] in the amount of $ ________________.

_____ We find in favor of defendant [*name*] and against plaintiff [*name*].

Signed: ___________________________
Presiding Juror

DATED:______________

After this verdict has [or, *all verdict forms have*] been signed, deliver this verdict form to the [*clerk* or *bailiff* or *judge*].

Form 10. Sample General Verdict Form

From CACI No. VF-5001 - General Verdict Form - Single Plaintiff Single Defendant - Multiple Causes of Action.

SUPERIOR COURT OF CALIFORNIA

COUNTY OF __________

______________________,	)	CASE NO. ______________
	)	
Plaintiff,	)	Assigned for all purposes to:
	)	Judge [*name*]
vs.	)	Dept. No. ____
	)	
______________________,	)	**GENERAL VERDICT**
	)	
Defendant.	)	
	)	
________________________________	)	

We, the jury in the above-entitled action, having determined our general verdict, find as follows:

For each claim, select one of the two options listed:

1. On plaintiff's First Cause of Action for Breach of Contract:

_____ We find in favor of plaintiff [*name*] and against defendant [*name*].

_____ We find in favor of defendant [*name*] and against plaintiff [*name*].

2. On plaintiff's Second Cause of Action for Breach of Warranty:

_____ We find in favor of plaintiff [*name*] and against defendant [*name*].

_____ We find in favor of defendant [*name*] and against plaintiff [*name*].

Complete the section below only if you find in favor of plaintiff [*name*] on at least one of [*his/her/its*] claims.

We award [*plaintiff*][*name*] the following damages: $_______________

Signed: ________________________
Presiding Juror

DATED:______________

After this verdict has [or, *all verdict forms have*] been signed, deliver this verdict form to the [*clerk* or *bailiff* or *judge*].

Form 11. Sample General Verdict Form

From CACI No. VF-5001 - General Verdict Form - Single Plaintiff Multiple Defendants - Multiple Causes of Action.

SUPERIOR COURT OF CALIFORNIA

COUNTY OF __________

________________________,	)	CASE NO. _______________
	)	
Plaintiff,	)	Assigned for all purposes to:
	)	Judge [*name*]
vs.	)	Dept. No. ____
	)	
________________________,	)	**GENERAL VERDICT**
	)	
Defendant.	)	
	)	
________________________________	)	

We, the jury in the above-entitled action, having determined our general verdict, find as follows:

For each claim, select one of the two options listed:

1. On plaintiff's First Cause of Action for Breach of Contract:

_____ We find in favor of plaintiff [*name*] and against defendant [*name*]. We further find in favor of plaintiff [*name*] and against defendant [*name*].

_____ We find in favor of defendant [*name*] and against plaintiff [*name*]. We further find in favor of defendant [*name*] and against plaintiff [*name*].

_____ We find in favor of plaintiff [*name*] and against defendant [*name*]. We further find in favor of defendant [*name*] and against plaintiff [*name*].

2. On plaintiff's Second Cause of Action for Breach of Warranty:

_____ We find in favor of plaintiff [*name*] and against defendant [*name*]. We further find in favor of plaintiff [*name*] and against defendant [*name*].

_____ We find in favor of defendant [*name*] and against plaintiff [*name*]. We further find in favor of defendant [*name*] and against plaintiff [*name*].

_____ We find in favor of plaintiff [*name*] and against defendant [*name*]. We further find in favor of defendant [*name*] and against plaintiff [*name*].

Complete the section below only if you find in favor of plaintiff [*name*] on at least one of [*his/her/its*] claims.

We award [*plaintiff*][*name*] the following damages: $_______________

Signed: ________________________
Presiding Juror

DATED:_____________

After this verdict has [or, *all verdict forms have*] been signed, deliver this verdict form to the [*clerk* or *bailiff* or *judge*].

Form 12. Sample General Verdict with Special Findings

SUPERIOR COURT OF CALIFORNIA

COUNTY OF __________

______________________,	)	CASE NO. ______________
	)	
Plaintiff,	)	Assigned for all purposes to:
	)	Judge [*name*]
vs.	)	Dept. No. ____
	)	
______________________,	)	**GENERAL VERDICT WITH**
	)	**SPECIAL FINDINGS**
Defendant.	)	
	)	
________________________________	)	

We, the jury in the above-entitled action, having determined our general verdict, find the following in response to the special interrogatories submitted to us:

1. Was [*defendant*] negligent?

Answer: Yes _____ No _______

If you answered "no" to Question No. 1, sign and return this verdict.

If you answered "yes" to Question No. 1, answer Question No. 2.

2. Was the negligence of [*defendant*] a proximate/legal cause of injury to [*plaintiff*]?

If you answered "no" to Question No. 2, sign and return this verdict.

If you answered "yes" to Question No. 2, answer Question No. 3.

3. What is the total amount of damages suffered by [*plaintiff*] as a result of the accident?

Answer: $ ______________.

Signed: ________________________
Presiding Juror

DATED: ________________

After this verdict has [or, *all verdict forms have*] been signed, deliver this verdict form to the [*clerk* or *bailiff* or *judge*].

Form 13. Sample Special Verdict Form

SUPERIOR COURT OF CALIFORNIA

COUNTY OF __________

______________________,	)	CASE NO. ______________
	)	
Plaintiff,	)	Assigned for all purposes to:
	)	Judge [*name*]
vs.	)	Dept. No. ____
	)	
______________________,	)	**SPECIAL VERDICT FORM**
	)	
Defendant.	)	
	)	
________________________________	)	

We, the jury in the above-entitled action, find the following special verdict on the questions submitted to us:

1. **Were any of the defendants negligent?** Answer "yes" or "no" after each defendant's name.

Defendant [*name*]	Yes ______	No _______
Defendant [*name*]	Yes ______	No _______
Defendant [*name*]	Yes ______	No _______

If you answered "no" to Question No. 1 as to all defendants, sign and return this verdict. No further questions should be answered. If you answered "yes" to Question No. 1 as to any defendant, then answer Question No. 2.

2. For each defendant for whom you answered "yes" in response to Question No. 2, was such negligence a cause of injury to the plaintiff? (Enter the defendant's name when your answer to Question No. 1 was "yes" and answer "yes" or "no" after each such defendant's name.)

Defendant [*name*] Yes ______ No ______

Defendant [*name*] Yes ______ No ______

Defendant [*name*] Yes ______ No ______

If you answered "no" to Question No. 2 as to all defendants listed there, sign and return this verdict form. No further questions should be answered. If you answered "yes" to Question No. 2 as to any defendant, then answer Question No. 3.

3. Without taking into consideration the reduction of damages due to the plaintiff's negligence, if any, what do you find to be the total amount of damages, including economic and noneconomic damages, if any suffered by the plaintiff and caused by the accident involved in this case?

(a) Economic damages: $__________

(b) Noneconomic Damages: $__________

TOTAL: $__________

If you answered "no damage" or "zero" to Question No. 3, sign and return this verdict. No further questions should be answered. If you answered Question No. 3 with an amount of money, answer Question No. 4.

4. Was the plaintiff negligent?

Yes _____ No _______

If you answered "no" to Question No. 4, do not answer Question No. 5. Instead, go directly to Question No. 6. If you answered "yes" to Question No. 4, answer Question No. 5.

5. Was the plaintiff's negligence a cause of any damage to the plaintiff?

Yes _____ No _______

6. Assuming that 100% represents the total negligence that was the cause of the plaintiff's damage, what percentage of this 100% is due to plaintiff's contributory negligence and what percentage of this 100% is due to the negligence of the defendant(s) and all other persons?

To plaintiff:	_________%
To defendant [*name*]:	_________%
To defendant [*name*]:	_________%
Other person(s) [*name(s)*]:	_________%
Other person(s) [*name(s)*]:	_________%

Signed: ___________________________
Presiding Juror

DATED: _________________

After this verdict has [or, *all verdict forms have*] been signed, deliver this verdict form to the [*clerk* or *bailiff* or *judge*].

Form 14. Sample breakdown of damages:

(a) **Past economic damages:**

Lost Earnings:	**$** ______________
Lost Profits:	**$**______________
Medical Expenses:	**$** ______________
Other past economic loss:	**$** ______________
Total Past Economic Damages:	**$**______________

(b) **Future Economic Loss:**

Future Earnings:	**$** ______________
Future Profits:	**$**______________
Future Medical Expenses:	**$** ______________
Other future economic loss:	**$** ______________
Total Future Economic Damages:	**$**______________

(c) **Past noneconomic loss, including**

[*physical pain, mental suffering*]: **$** ______________

(d) **Future noneconomic loss, including**

[*physical pain, mental suffering*]: **$** ______________

Form 15. Sample Verdict with Special Findings regarding Punitive Damages

SUPERIOR COURT OF CALIFORNIA

COUNTY OF __________

______________________,	)	CASE NO. _______________
	)	
Plaintiff,	)	Assigned for all purposes to:
	)	Judge [*name*]
vs.	)	Dept. No. ____
	)	
______________________,	)	**VERDICT WITH SPECIAL**
	)	**FINDINGS REGARDING**
Defendant.	)	**PUNITIVE DAMAGES**
	)	
______________________________	)	

We, the jury in the above-entitled action, find for the [*party*] [*name*] and against the [*party*][*name*] [*if for plaintiff*: in the sum of $________ as actual damages].

We further find in answer to the special interrogatories submitted to us as follows:

ISSUE NO. 1: If you found that plaintiff [*name*] was entitled to recover actual damages against defendant [*name*], was defendant [*name*] guilty of oppression, fraud, or malice in doing the acts that caused plaintiff's actual damages?

Answer "yes" or "no."

ANSWER: _______

ISSUE NO. 2: If you answered Issue No. 1 yes, what amount of punitive damages, if any, do you assess against defendant [*name*] for the sake of example and by way of punishment?

ANSWER: Amount of Punitive Damages: $______________

DATED:______________

Signed: __________________________
Presiding Juror

After this verdict has [or, *all verdict forms have*] been signed, deliver this verdict form to the [*clerk* or *bailiff* or *judge*].

(**Note:** See CACI for sample verdict forms for causes of actions that allow punitive damages.)

Appendix D

Forms for Judgments

Form 16. Sample Judgment after Bench Trial

[*Name of attorney with Bar number*]
[*Address*]
[*Telephone*]
[*Fax number*]
[*E-mail, if appropriate*]

Attorney for [*Party*] [*name*]

SUPERIOR COURT OF CALIFORNIA

COUNTY OF ___________

________________________,	)	CASE NO. _______________
	)	
Plaintiff,	)	Assigned for all purposes to:
	)	Judge [name]
vs.	)	Dept. No. ____
	)	
________________________,	)	**PROPOSED JUDGMENT**
	)	
Defendant.	)	Complaint filed:
	)	Trial date:
________________________________	)	

The above-entitled action came on regularly for hearing on [*date*] at [*time*] in Department No. __ before the Honorable [*name*], Judge Presiding, sitting without a jury. The parties waived a jury trial. Plaintiff, [*name*], appeared by [*his/her/its*] attorney, [*name*]. Defendant, [*name*], appeared by [*his/her/its*] attorney, [*name*].

Oral and documentary evidence was introduced on half of the parties. The cause was argued and submitted to the Court for decision. The Court, having considered the evidence and heard the arguments of counsel, and being fully advised, and a Statement of Decision [*not*] having been requested,

IT IS ORDERED, ADJUDGED, AND DECREE THAT:

Plaintiff, [*name*], have judgment against defendant [*name*], for the following:

1. Damages in the sum of $_____________.

2. Prejudgment interest in the sum of $__________, computed at ____ percent per annum from [*date*].

3. Attorney's fees in the sum of $____________.

4. Costs in the sum of $_________.

OR

Plaintiff, [*name*], take nothing, with defendant, [*name*], to recover the following from plaintiff:

3. Attorney's fees in the sum of $____________.

4. Costs in the sum of $_________.

CONTINUE:

DATED: ______________

BY__________________________
Judge of the Superior Court

(***Note***: See also Judicial Council Form JUD-100 for a printed Judgment form.)

Form 17. Sample Judgment after Jury Trial using General Verdict Form

[*Name of attorney with Bar number*]
[*Address*]
[*Telephone*]
[*Fax number*]
[*E-mail, if appropriate*]

Attorney for [*Party*]

SUPERIOR COURT OF CALIFORNIA

COUNTY OF __________

______________________,)	CASE NO. ______________
Plaintiff,)	Assigned for all purposes to: Judge [*name*] Dept. No. ____
vs.)	
______________________,)	**PROPOSED JUDGMENT**
Defendant.)	Complaint filed: Trial date:

The above-entitled action came on regularly for hearing on [*date*] at [*time*] in Department No. __ before the Honorable [*name*], Judge Presiding. Plaintiff, [*name*], appeared by [*his/her/its*] attorney, [*name*]. Defendant, [*name*], appeared by [*his/her/its*] attorney, [*name*].

A jury of 12 persons was regularly impaneled and sworn to try the action. Witnesses on the part of the plaintiff and the defendants were sworn and examined. After hearing the evidence, the arguments of counsel and instructions of the Court, the jury deliberated and thereafter returned into Court with its verdict as follows:

Plaintiff [*name*] is entitled to judgment against defendant [*name*] in the amount of $______________.

It appearing by reason of said verdict that: plaintiff [*name*] is entitled to judgment against defendant [*name*].

NOW, THEREFORE, IT IS ORDERED, ADJUDGED AND DECREED that said plaintiff [*name*] recorder from defendant [*name*] the sum of $_______, with interest thereon at the rate of ten (10%) percent per annum from the date of the entry of this judgment until paid, together with costs in the amount of $__________.

DATED: _______________

BY__________________________
Judge of the Superior Court

Form 18. Sample Judgment after Jury Trial using General Verdict Form with Special Interrogatories

[*Name of attorney with Bar number*]
[*Address*]
[*Telephone*]
[*Fax number*]
[*E-mail, if appropriate*]

Attorney for [*Party*]

SUPERIOR COURT OF CALIFORNIA

COUNTY OF __________

________________________,	) CASE NO. ______________
	)
Plaintiff,	) Assigned for all purposes to:
	) Judge [*name*]
vs.	) Dept. No. ____
	)
________________________,	) **PROPOSED JUDGMENT**
	)
Defendant.	) Complaint filed:
	) Trial date:
________________________________	)

The above-entitled action came on regularly for hearing on [*date*] at [*time*] in Department No. __ before the Honorable [*name*], Judge Presiding. Plaintiff, [*name*], appeared by [*his/her/its*] attorney, [*name*]. Defendant, [*name*], appeared by [*his/her/its*] attorney, [*name*].

A jury of 12 persons was regularly impaneled and sworn to try the action. Witnesses on the part of the plaintiff and the defendants were sworn and examined. After hearing the evidence, the arguments of counsel and instructions of the Court, the jury retired to consider a general verdict on special interrogatories. The jury deliberated and thereafter returned into Court and being called, the jurors answered to their names and rendered their verdict in writing in words and figures as follows:

IT IS ORDERED, ADJUDGED, AND DECREED THAT:

Plaintiff, [*name*] recover judgment against defendant, [*name*], in the amount of $__________, with interest thereon at the legal rate of ten (10%) percent per annum from the date of entry of this judgment until paid; and

Plaintiff, [*name*], recover against defendant, [*name*], costs in the amount of $________________.

OR

Plaintiff, [*name*], recover nothing from defendant, [*name*]; and

Defendant, [*name*], recover against plaintiff, [*name*], costs in the amount of $ ____________.

NOW, THEREFORE, IT IS ORDERED, ADJUDGED, AND DECREED:

Plaintiff, [*name*], have judgment against defendant, [*name*], in the sum of $_______ with interest thereon at the rate of % per annum [date] to the date of this judgment in the amount of $____, plus costs incurred by plaintiff in the sum of $ _________.

OR

Defendant, [*name*], is entitled to judgment against plaintiff, [*name*], and plaintiff [*name*] shall take nothing.

AND

That [*plaintiff* or *defendant*], [*name*], recover costs and disbursements taxed in the sum of $ _________.

DATED: ______________

BY________________________
Judge of the Superior Court

Form 19. Sample Judgment after Jury Trial using Special Verdict Form

[*Name of attorney with Bar number*]
[*Address*]
[*Telephone*]
[*Fax number*]
[*E-mail, if appropriate*]

Attorney for [*Party*]

SUPERIOR COURT OF CALIFORNIA

COUNTY OF __________

______________________,	CASE NO. ______________
Plaintiff,	Assigned for all purposes to: Judge [*name*] Dept. No. ____
vs.	
______________________,	**PROPOSED JUDGMENT**
Defendant.	Complaint filed: Trial date:

The above-entitled action came on regularly for hearing on [*date*] at [*time*] in Department No. __ before the Honorable [*name*], Judge Presiding. Plaintiff, [*name*], appeared by [*his/her/its*] attorney, [*name*]. Defendant, [*name*], appeared by [*his/her/its*] attorney, [*name*].

A jury of 12 persons was regularly impaneled and sworn to try the action. Witnesses on the part of the plaintiff and the defendants were sworn and examined. After hearing the evidence, the arguments of counsel and instructions of the Court, the jury retired to consider a verdict on special issues. The jury deliberated and thereafter returned into Court with its verdict consisting of the special issues submitted to the jury and the answers given thereto by the jury, which said verdict was filed with the clerk and entered upon the minutes, and the jurors answered to their names and rendered their verdict in words and figures as follows:

(*Quote the entire special verdict* verbatim, including the following language.)

We, the jury in the above-entitled action, find the following Special Verdicts on the issues submitted to us:

ISSUE: ____

ANSWER: ____

ISSUE: ____

ANSWER: ____

ISSUE: ____

ANSWER: ____

ISSUE: ____

ANSWER: ____

It appearing that by reason of said special verdict:

[Describe judgment, e.g., defendant [*name*] is legally obligated to pay plaintiff [*name*] the sum of $________, plus interest at the rate of ____ % per annum from [*date*] to the date of this judgment in the amount of $____, plus costs incurred by plaintiff in the sum of $ _________.]

OR

Defendant [*name*] is entitled to judgment against plaintiff [*name*], and plaintiff [*name*] shall take nothing.

NOW, THEREFORE, IT IS ORDERED, ADJUDGED, AND DECREED:

Plaintiff [*name*] have judgment against defendant [*name*] in the sum of $________ with interest thereon at the rate of % per annum [date] to the date of this judgment in the amount of $____, plus costs incurred by plaintiff [*name*] in the sum of $ _________.

OR

Defendant [*name*] is entitled to judgment against plaintiff [*name*], and plaintiff [*name*] shall take nothing.

AND

That [*plaintiff* or *defendant*] [*name*] recover costs and disbursements taxed in the sum of $ _________.

DATED: ______________

BY__________________________
Judge of the Superior Court

Form 20. Sample Notice of Entry of Judgment Form

[*Name of attorney with Bar number*]
[*Address*]
[*Telephone*]
[*Fax number*]
[*E-mail, if appropriate*]

Attorney for [*Party*] [*name*]

SUPERIOR COURT OF CALIFORNIA

COUNTY OF __________

<table>
<tr><td>______________________,

Plaintiff,

vs.

______________________,

Defendant.
________________________________</td><td>)
)
)
)
)
)
)
)
)
)
)</td><td>CASE NO. ______________

Assigned for all purposes to:
Judge [name]
Dept. No. ____

NOTICE OF ENTRY OF JUDGMENT

Complaint filed:
Trial Date:</td></tr>
</table>

TO: ALL PARTIES AND THEIR ATTORNEYS OF RECORD:

Notice is hereby given that on [*date*], judgment was entered in favor of plaintiff [*name*], and against defendant [*name*], in the amount of $ ________ . A copy of the judgment is attached hereto.

DATED: ______________

BY___________________________
[*Attorney's name*]
Attorney for [*party*] [*name*]

(**Note:** See also preprinted Judicial Council Form, No. CIV-130.)

Appendix E

Forms for Notice of Intention to Move for New Trial

Form 21. Sample Notice of Intention to Move for New Trial

[*Name of attorney with Bar number*]
[*Address*]
[*Telephone*]
[*Fax number*]
[*E-mail, if appropriate*]

Attorney for [*Party*] [*name*]

SUPERIOR COURT OF CALIFORNIA

COUNTY OF __________

______________________,	)	CASE NO. ______________
	)	
Plaintiff,	)	Assigned for all purposes to:
	)	Judge [*name*]
vs.	)	Dept. No. ____
	)	
______________________,	)	**NOTICE OF INTENTION**
	)	**TO MOVE FOR NEW TRIAL**
Defendant.	)	
	)	Complaint filed:
________________________________	)	Trial Date:

TO: ALL PARTIES AND THEIR ATTORNEYS OF RECORD:

Notice is hereby given that on [*date*] at [*time*], or as soon thereafter as this matter can be heard, in Department No. ___ of the above-entitled Court, located at [*address*], [*plaintiff/defendant*] [*name*] intends to move this Court to vacate and set aside the verdict of the jury and judgment entered thereon rendered in favor of [*plaintiff/defendant*] [*name*] and against [*plaintiff/defendant*] [*name*] and to grant [*plaintiff/defendant*] [*name*] a new trial on the following grounds:

[*Set forth all statutory grounds that may apply and as listed in Code of Civil Procedure section* ___]

With respect to grounds [*list*], set forth above, this motion will be made on affidavits or declarations to be submitted; with respect to grounds [*list*], this motion will be made on the minutes of the Court.

This motion will also be based upon this Notice, the memorandum of points and authorities to be served and filed hereafter, the pleadings, the records and filed herein, such matters as to which this Court may take judicial notice, and on such oral argument as this Court allows.

DATED: _______________

BY___________________________

[*Attorney's name*]
Attorney for [*Party*] [*name*]

Table of Authorities

CASES:

CONSTITUTION, STATUTES, AND RULES:

TREATISES:

INDEX

A

B

C

D

E

F

G

H

I

J

T

U

V

W

Y

Afterword

When I first began to specialize in appellate law in 1980, trial attorneys rarely called on appellate attorneys until after the trial proceedings were at an end. By then the record was set.

Trial lawyers have gotten more savvy since those early days. The modern trend is to involve appellate attorneys at the earlier stages of dispositive motions or trial. Smart thinking! I commend trial attorneys for taking this extra step to protect their cases and hope more will adopt this practice. It could make the difference between winning or losing.

Of course, every trial lawyer would love to win his or her case and have the opposing party recognize the futility of appealing. But, even with our best efforts, it doesn't always happen that way. This book gives you the strategic tools necessary for the appellate attorney to continue on with the fight.

Hopefully, this book will continue to grow, and you can be part of that process. I have discussed the common errors that I have encountered through my years of practice. If you've encountered different problems, I'd like to know about them. You can help me add to my knowledge by sharing your stories (good and bad) by:

- **Email:** Send your comments and recommendations to me at Donna@DonnaBader.com.

- **Blog:** Follow my blog at www.AnAppealtoReason.com, which will continue to cover the topics addressed in this book. Feel free to make your comments and share your stories there as well. If you have questions, I will try to spotlight them in future blogs.

- **Facebook:** Follow me on Facebook at Facebook.com/Bench Press Publishing.

- **Write:** Send me a letter at 668 North Coast Highway, Ste. 1355, Laguna Beach, California 92651. Yes, I still read mail the old-fashioned way.

- **Call:** Give me a call at (949) 494-7455.

- **Updates:** As we continue to share our knowledge and experience, this book may be updated to reflect new information and cases.